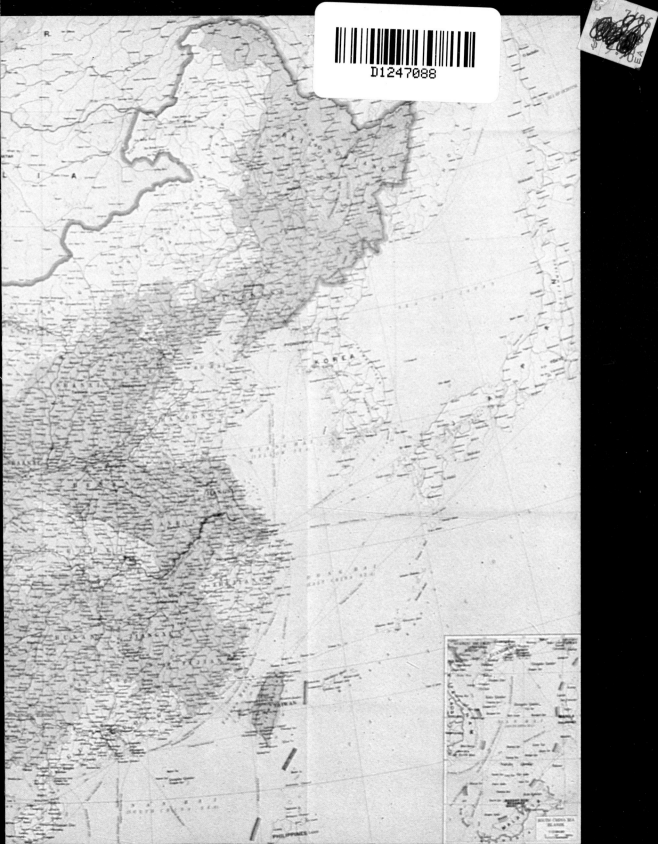

To China for Steam

To China for Steam

Robert Adley

BLANDFORD PRESS
POOLE · DORSET

Books by the same author

British Steam in Cameracolour (Ian Allen)
In Search of Steam
Call of Steam

First published in the U.K. 1983, by Blandford Press
Link House, West Street, Poole, Dorset, BH15 1LL
Copyright © 1983 Robert Adley

British Library Cataloguing in Publication Data

Adley, Robert
  To China for steam.
  1. Locomotives—China
  I. Title
  625.2'61'0951   TJ603.4.C6

Typeset by Keyspools Ltd, Golborne,
Lancs.

Printed in Hong Kong by Lee-Fung Asco

Contents

Dedication

To Emperor Qin Shi Huang, who first unified China, and who, for all his faults, would doubtless have built a national railway network in 221 BC if the steam-engine had been invented. Also to Jane, who was not alive in 221 BC, but who has had to live with my railway enthusiasm for what must seem an eternity.

Finally, to the people of China, whose turbulent history has forced them to endure so much. They have triumphed over adversity, face the future with hope and may yet become a nation of railway enthusiasts, if I may assess their interest in the subject of my hobby, by measuring their friendliness towards me.

Introduction

What is a railway enthusiast? Why does the steam locomotive arouse such emotion, affection and enduring admiration amongst certain people? Over the years, many have sought to answer this question, but few have succeeded. Of one thing I am certain, however: there is a Brotherhood of Rail. It knows neither national, ethnic nor cultural boundaries. It binds together peasant and philosopher, communist and capitalist, male and female. I offer you this book, kind reader, as a contribution towards the worldwide lasting tribute to the steam engine. For steam enthusiasts, for members of the Brotherhood of Rail, the place to go is to China, for steam.

Around the world, for good or evil, my fellow-countrymen have left their mark, not always at the behest of the local inhabitants. That 'mark' is superbly illustrated by the Ordnance Survey Maps of China, made in Southampton; but more of that later. However, having invented the steam-engine, I suppose its worship is one of our less harmful attributes. It is not my deliberate intention to seek, through this book, to gain new adherents to the cause of railway enthusiasm: or is it? Can I put my hand on my heart and express no interest in strengthening the international army of the Brotherhood of Rail? No, I cannot. Of course I hope that army grows in number, not because I hope to sell more books, but because I believe in railways. For a land that believes in railways it is unnecessary to look further than the People's Republic of China.

In spite of the scale of development of the Chinese People's Republic Railways (CPRR), the Vice President of Railways, Liao Shiquan has stated that progress can barely keep pace with the growing demands made on the railways by the growth of the national economy and foreign trade. Steam traction still has a part to play in the development of CPRR. In the late 1950s, about 1,000 second-hand Soviet 'FD' class steam locomotives were delivered to China. These locomotives, of modern design and of 2–10–2

Overleaf
Photographing the sunset on a tropical island, with palm trees framing gentle waves, is easy. Finding somewhere in China where a railway runs between an accessible camera location and hills behind which the sun will set and then hoping that a steam-hauled train will appear, is quite a task. The first essential is an interpreter who understands one's requirements. Secondly, one needs a local guide with detailed knowledge of railway lines. Thirdly, one needs a clear sky and also one needs luck. Near Fenhe, a few miles from Taiyuan, on 1 November 1982, the ingredients almost came together. Lacking the unreal glamour of 'fixed' photography, 'QJ' class 2–10–2 No. 3125, tender-first, heads an eastbound freight. In my life, time is the most scarce ingredient . . .

wheel arrangement, replaced large numbers of elderly locomotives. The Russians, at that time, helped the Chinese with the
design and introduction of an even more powerful 2–10–2
locomotive, formerly called the 'Heping' (Peace) class, the first
prototype of which was assembled at Lüda (Dalian) in 1956. In
serial production by 1959, the 'QJ' class, as they are now known,
is still in production, at Datong, at the last locomotive works in
the world still series-building steam engines. The 'QJ' is an
excellent locomotive, ably and amply fulfilling its design criteria,
and playing a vital part in an expanding railway system.

   Travel by train is safe, friendly and, in China, efficient. You
meet people. There is neither the tension, the interminable
waiting, nor the impersonality of the aeroplane, nor is there the
disagreeable competitiveness, not to mention the danger, of the
road. Trains and railways are for, of and about people. They are
alive. Yet the railway, over the years, has meant more than just
jobs and transport.

   The Railway Protection League, founded in Chengdu, in
Sichuan Sheng (Province) on 17 June 1911, was by no means a
Chinese version of the Railway Correspondence and Travel
Society: it was a political organization, established to pressurise
the Government in Beijing, and which ignited the spark of

One of Zhengzhou North
Shed's 107 'QJ' class 2–10–2s,
No. 2880, had been prepared
and was immaculate for my
visit on 2 November 1982.
The QJ's cab is immense by
comparison with the cab of
any British steam locomotive.
To climb aboard, as shown,
needed the assistance of at
least one person to carry two
or three cameras, camera
case, tripod and tripod bag,
but everybody was always
immensely helpful.

10

As one of the first western Parliamentarians to visit the People's Republic, in 1973, my mind was far from steam-engines as we were taken to visit the Great Wall. Our convoy of cars was halted at a level-crossing and the sight of a steam-hauled train caused me to jump out of the car and run to the barrier, camera in hand. Here then is the first photograph of steam that I took in China; a 'QJ' 2–10–2 banking a freight up towards Badaling, not far from the Great Wall.

political contest and struggle between central and provincial authority. The League's leader, P'u Tien-chun was jailed; there was an uprising in Sichuan, and eventually the year 1911 was proudly marked in blood in China's history. I have failed to resist the temptation occasionally to sprinkle history, and indeed historic maps, throughout this book, for which I do not apologize.

From 1876 to 1949, only 21,000 kilometres of railway were built in that vast country. By the time of liberation in 1949, only 11,000 kilometres of line were still open to traffic, the remainder having been destroyed by years of internal conflict and disorder.

Progress since 1949 has been substantial, with some of the lines being built through terrain that would have daunted a less determined nation. The total rail system now exceeds 51,000 kilometres, whilst many single track sections have been doubled. Before 1949, seven provinces were without railways altogether, including Sichuan, scene of the formation of the Railway Protection League. Now only the autonomous Province of Xizang Zizhiqu (Tibet) is without railway communication, the railway reaching the populous but remote province of Sichuan in 1952 with the completion of the Chengdu-Chongqing line. The line to Lhasa is under construction.

Searching for nuggets of history to accompany the photographs and to incorporate within various chapters of this book, has opened up, for me, a fascinating world – the world of China's railway history. My research has tended to highlight the dearth of information of this rich but not well-documented seam of history.

The House of Commons Library recommended two useful sources: *Foreign Investment & Economic Development in China 1840–1937*: and *China's Quest for Railway Autonomy 1904–1911*. The latter, subtitled *A Study of the Chinese Railway-Rights Recovery Movement*, and written by Lee En Han, is a gem. As its subtitle indicates, however, it deals primarily with the political and economic aspects of what is necessarily a specialist subject. As the author says in the first sentence of his preface 'This study of the Chinese railway rights recovery movement of the early twentieth century is part of an overall research on the development of Chinese modern nationalism, which is considered the most forceful ideology to have influenced Chinese society in modern times'. Published in 1977, Lee En Han's book is the nearest I have come to a 'Railway History' book, but it is an altogether different tome to the innumerable books published in Britain during the last 150 years, of historic record and documentation of individual lines, of the railway companies, of the locomotives and of the great engineers. It is no criticism of Lee En Han's book to say that it contains no photographs at all – of locomotives, of places, of railway buildings or of people connected with the railways, but it was valuable indeed to me as it introduced me to that unexpected source of late night pleasure in the House of Commons Library, in the shape of the Commercial Reports from His Majesty's Minister at Peking, and from Her Majesty's and His Majesty's Consuls at various Chinese cities, between 1866 and 1916. Late night sittings were transformed as I pored over fascinating and sometimes seemingly unopened volumes, instead of poring over a whisky in the smoking room.

My greatest 'discovery', if he will excuse the word, was to meet and talk to Lt. Col. Kenneth Cantlie, President of The China Society: a remarkable man, whose modesty belies his knowledge and his achievements, and who deserves more than a passing mention in this 'Introduction'. He is entitled to a full chapter, which is called 'Friend of Sun Yat Sen' (Chapter 5). For a concise lesson in China's railway history and geography, his booklet, *The Railways of China*, is invaluable.

For those unfamiliar with the geography of China, I have included some general maps. Maps are to railway enthusiasts what a compass is to an explorer. When I started to write this book, I knew that I should need maps. In my last two books, *In Search of Steam* and *The Call of Steam*, my friends at the Ordnance

Searching for steam in China, whilst a member of a Parliamentary delegation, often means frustration caused by lack of time, either to 'escape' from the delegation's itinerary or to find and visit fruitful locations. A distant sight of wisps of steam, or a glimpse of an engine which never comes nearer, can be agonizing. This agony and frustration is illustrated here, in a picture I caption 'Lurking at the Gate', at Nankou. This place is on the first railway line in the country to be built entirely under Chinese auspices. It runs from Beijing, up through the 'Western Hills' separating the alluvial plane of North China from the undulating tableland of Mongolia. The line is now extensively used by tourists to the Great Wall. The locomotive is almost certainly a Japanese-built 'JF$_6$' class 2–8–2: its number is 3413: the date is 12 March 1982.

Survey (OS), in Southampton, opened up their archives to reveal a wealth of old maps which helped me to trace and to illustrate the impact of railways on Britain's landscape. They added an extra dimension to my books. In my ignorance I did not realise the wealth of maps of China emanating from the same source. Indeed, this knowledge came to me whilst scouring the Accounts and Papers in the Library at the House of Commons, which have given me ideas above my station, (excuse the railwayism!) as a trainee railway historian. These maps, accompanying the Commercial Reports from Her Majesty's and later His Majesty's Consuls are, quite simply, fascinating. My searches for maps introduced me to many helpful and most interesting people, amongst whom I must mention Dr. Helen Wallis at the British Library, George Hardy at the Royal Geographical Society (RGS) and Peter Clarke at the Ministry Defence. (MOD)

To my surprise and dismay, however, Ordnance Survey at Southampton could find no record of their maps of China, although Alan Marles, at this establishment, introduced me to the redoubtable but captivating Helen Wallis. I tried the Foreign Office and was referred to the Ministry of Defence which opened the magic box. In a small office, in an uninspiring single-storey building in a London suburb, were the original copies of scores of

13

old maps of China, dating from the closing years of the last century to the early years of this. Searching hungrily through the old records was a marvellous experience. Many of the original maps were noted as having been transferred to the Royal Geographical Society in 1921/22. To the RGS., who opened up their archives for me, to the British Library and to the MOD, I owe a debt of considerable thanks.

Old maps, charts and documents vividly illustrate the political, economic and military penetration of, and interference with China's affairs, practised by foreign powers: not just by my forebears, but by French and German, Belgian and Danish, American and Russian, let alone by the aggressive Japanese who mercilessly exploited the Chinese.

Spanning the period from the date of construction, by a British company, of the first railway in China, in 1876, to the period up to and just beyond the effective nationalization of the railways, in 1911, the Parliamentary Accounts and Papers and their accompanying maps tell so much more about contemporary China than merely details of the progress of the planning and construction of sections of railway line. This is not a history book so I have not included this material. Perhaps it needs another on China's railway history: Publisher, please note!

There remains an unfilled gap in the detailed railway history of China, between the revolutions, from 1911 to 1949, but some of it is charted by Kenneth Cantlie in *Railways of China*.

With rebuilding and new building since 1949, it has become a modern railway, notwithstanding steam, which only its detractors would claim to be outdated. China's railway signalling system is mainly modern and sophisticated, making much of British Rail's equipment seem quaint. Do not bother to go to China to see semaphore signals: go to Cornwall or Yorkshire. If there are any politicians in the People's Republic who are hostile towards investment in the railways, they are less successful than their British contemporaries.

Let my next point of railway history relate to the memory of the engineer who built the first Chinese railway, Zhan Tianyou. The contribution of this outstanding man was immense. In 1905 he designed and had built the Beijing-Zhangjiakou (Kalgan) Railway, the first in China to be designed and built completely by Chinese. The 200 kilometre line presented difficult engineering problems, including the tunnelling of 1,646 metres through rocky mountains north-west of Beijing. The line was completed two years ahead of schedule. Extended on to Datong, this line became one of the main spokes of the railway system radiating from Beijing.

Zhan Tianyou invented the automatic coupling. On the IPU

'RM' class 4–6–2 No. 1014 has charge of a heavy eastbound train at North Gate, Xian, on 4 November 1982. The water-tower is a prominent feature of the Chinese landscape, as is the urban haze and the pedestrians walking beside the track. At this date, Xian was 100 per cent steam, with the 'RM' Pacifics predominant on passenger trains. Long may they reign!

delegation visit to China in the spring of 1982, I used to drink a toast to him, coupled with the name of James Watt. This seemed to please our hosts.

Everywhere I went in China to photograph steam, I was met with friendly inquisitiveness. How strange I must have looked. Yet the Chinese reaction to my odd hobby was always sympathetic. At each chosen location they could see what I was doing and what I was trying to achieve.

Concern for my safety must have caused heartache to my hosts from time to time. For this, I can only apologize. To my colleagues on Parliamentary delegations, whose movements I sometimes manipulated, my apologies too. Yet in truth, railway photography in the People's Republic brings pleasure, not anguish, to both photographer and subject. 'Friendship' is just a word. Politicians trade in words. After-dinner speeches, formal meetings, fine phrases, and pontificating sentiments, fill our lives. Yet 'friendship' is personal – between people, as individuals. The wave of a cheerful Chinese engine driver does more, for me, than a hundred fine speeches.

This is my fourth railway book. All the words and photographs are mine. Whereas the three previous books feature steam-engines in Britain, this book features only locomotives in

China. My British photographs were taken between 1962 and 1968. My Chinese photographs were taken during three visits to the People's Republic, in 1973 and twice during 1982. As in Britain, I owe innumerable debts of thanks to those who helped me, indeed who enabled me to take the photographs. Whereas Britain's railway authorities have lived for more than a century with railway enthusiasts and photographers, the breed is comparatively new in China. For this reason, please excuse a few further words of explanation.

Railways and steam-engines, have their own language. My British railway enthusiast readers must bear with me for a moment if I address a few remarks to those who have not yet joined our 'club', for my visit to China in Autumn 1982 was a visit with the sole purpose of taking photographs for this book. During my ten hectic days, it quickly became clear that translation of technical terminology presented my Chinese friends with unusual problems.

Take the word 'class' for example. Any British railway enthusiast knows the difference between a 'Black Five' and a 'Hall', but what about the difference between a 'QJ' and a 'JF'? To run 'tender first', or 'light engine': to 'enter the shed' or 'double-head'. Merely to use such terms will, I hope, cause

The importance of Datong's coal resources was prophesied long ago (see Page 121). Coal is one of Datong's vital contributions to the Chinese economy and still fuels the transport that takes the 'black gold' from the region, to the corners of China. The spirit of steam is encapsulated by two modern 'QJ' class 2–10–2 locomotives powering a heavy coal train eastwards out of Datong, on the rising gradient to Julebu, on 31 October 1982.

China's greatest natural resource, is her people, probably millions of whom work on the railways. Beijing's last centre of steam activity is Fengtai, the earliest railway junction in China, and once the site of a strange confrontation between British and German troops. A permanent way gang work on the track, between simmering 'QJs', on 29 October 1982. There are stabling and servicing facilities here, but no steam-engines are permanently allocated any more. Fengtai sees mostly 'QJ' class 2–10–2s, with a sprinkling of 'JS' and 'JF' 2–8–2s.

railway enthusiasts to smile in trying to understand why it seems to me necessary to devote a page to notes of 'Terminology', mainly intended to help readers of the Chinese version of this book. To try to write a book that neither mystifies non-enthusiasts nor infuriates enthusiasts, is not an easy task.

I have to tackle the problem of language, too. The problem of the transliteration of Chinese place-names into Roman characters has been made more, and not less, difficult since the introduction of 'Pinyin' to replace the 'Wade-Giles' version, which itself was often different to traditional spelling. Of course, as one might expect, 'Wade-Giles' was written by an Englishman for the English-speaking, whilst 'Pinyin' was not: thus Chengchou or Chengchow has become Zhengzhou. On numerous world maps, such as may be seen in this book, many names were spelt in the 'traditional' English manner. Names like Canton, Tsingtao or Kalgan illustrate the problem thus:

Pinyin	Wade-Giles	Traditional
Guangzhou	Kuan-chou	Canton
Qingdao	Ching-tao	Tsingtao
Zhangjiakou	Chang-Chia-K'ou	Kalgan

In determining how to proceed in this book with a degree of uniformity, I have decided that good manners should be my guide. It is the Chinese language, and 'Pinyin' which is now their official standard transliteration; not translation, please note. Wherever possible, subject to my not being scholarly or even knowledgeable about the Chinese language, I have therefore used 'Pinyin' in the text. There is a glossary of the language of place-names on Page 151. Obviously, I have reproduced all maps as they exist, with the source of the information supplied. My lack of scholarship will be embarrasingly apparent: to be matched only by the humility of my apologies to those less ignorant than I. (*The Gazeteer of the People's Republic of China: Pinyin-Wade-Giles: Wade-Giles – Pinyin*, runs to 919 pages.)

Whilst books on the history of Britain's railways abound, there is a dearth of English language literature on the history of China's railways, as I have said. Here is a gap to be filled by someone academically more gifted than I. Indeed, it would be a superb subject to tackle. Notwithstanding the fact that China's first railway line was opened half a century after the world's first public railway to use steam power, the Stockton & Darlington in

Until I received the map, especially prepared for me by the China Railway Publishing House and illustrated on Page 20, my source of reference was a useful map prepared from information obtained by visiting railway enthusiasts, and produced by the Quail Map Company. Above is an extract. The map is in Wade-Giles, but a few important cities have Pinyin transliteration. Places in red relate to locations featured photographically in this book. On the facing page is the map which was prepared by the China Society for inclusion in Kenneth Cantlie's book (see Chapter 5). I am indebted to both Quail and the China Society for granting me permission to use these maps.

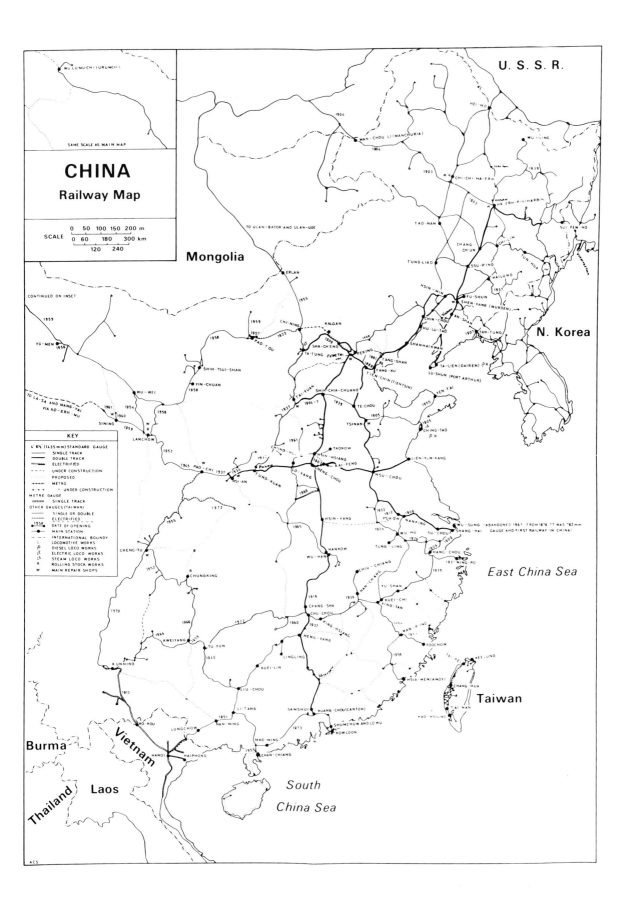

CHINA

Railway Map

SCALE

0	50	100	150	200 m
0	60	180	300 km

120   240

SAME SCALE AS MAIN MAP

KEY

4' 8½" (1435 mm) STANDARD GAUGE
────── SINGLE TRACK
══════ DOUBLE TRACK
▰▰▰▰▰▰ ELECTRIFIED
- - - - - UNDER CONSTRUCTION
·········· PROPOSED
+++++ METRO
+ + + " UNDER CONSTRUCTION
METRE GAUGE
▭▭▭▭▭ SINGLE TRACK
OTHER GAUGES (TAIWAN)
▱▱▱▱▱ SINGLE OR DOUBLE
▱▱▱▱▱ ELECTRIFIED _ _
1958 DATE OF OPENING
● MAIN STATION
─ ─ INTERNATIONAL BOUNDY
L LOCOMOTIVE WORKS
D DIESEL LOCO WORKS
LE ELECTRIC LOCO WORKS
LS STEAM LOCO WORKS
R ROLLING STOCK WORKS
W MAIN REPAIR SHOPS

U.S.S.R.

Mongolia

N. Korea

Burma

Vietnam

Thailand   **Laos**

Taiwan

East China Sea

South China Sea

TO ULAN-BATOR AND ULAN-UDE

CONTINUED ON INSET

TO LA-SA AND MANG-TAI
VIA KO-ERH-MU

WU-LU-MU-CHI (URUMCHI)

YU-MEN

SINING

WU-WEI

LANCHOW

SHIM-TSUI-SHAN

YIN-CHUAN

ERLAN

CHI-NING

PAO-TOU

KALGAN

SHA-CHENG

TA-TUNG

PEKING

TAI-YUAN

SHIH-CHIA-CHUANG

PAO-CHI

HSI-AN

TUNG-KUAN

CO-YANG

CHENG-CHOU

HSIN-HSIANG

TAOKOW

KAI-FENG

TE-CHOU

TSINAN

CHING-TAO

YEN-TAI

HSU-CHOU

LIEN-YUN-KANG

CHENG-TU

CHUNGKING

KWEIYANG

YU-YUN

KUNMING

HO-KOU

LUNGCHOW

NAN-NING

HAIPHONG

HANOI

MAO-MING

CHAN-CHIANG

LI-TANG

SAMSHUI

KUANG-CHOU (CANTON)

KOWLOON

SHUMCHUN AND LOWU

KWEI-LIN

LIU-CHOU

LINGLING

HENG-YANG

CHANG-SHA

CHU-CHOU

PING-HSIANG

NAN-CHANG

YU-SHAN

KUEI-CHI

YING-TAN

NAN-PING

FOOCHOW

HSIA-MEN (AMOY)

CHANG-HUA

TAI-NAN

KAO-HSIUNG

TAI-PEI

KEE-LUNG

NING-PO

HANG-CHOU

SHANG-HAI

SU-CHOU

WU-SUNG (ABANDONED 196? FROM 1876-77 WAS 762 mm GAUGE AND FIRST RAILWAY IN CHINA)

NAN-KING

PUKOW

WU-HU

TUNG-LING

WU-HAN

HANKOW

CHIU-CHIANG

HSIN-YANG

TIEN-CHIN (TIENTSIN)

TANG-KU

TANG-SHAN

FENGTAI Jet.

SHANHAIKWAN

LU-SHUN (PORT ARTHUR)

TA-LIEN (DAIREN) DR

AN-SHAN

MU-LU-TAO

SHEN-YANG (MUKDEN)

AN-TUNG

FU-SHUN

HSIN-MIN

TUNG-LIAO

SSU-PING

HAILUNG

CHI-LIN

TUN-HUA

CHANG-CHUN

HA-ERH-PIN (HARBIN)

TAO-NAN

CHI-CHI-HA-ERH

MAN-CHOU-LI (MANCHURIA)

HEI-HO

WU-I-LING

SUI-FEN-HO

1904

1903

1959

1958

1957

1959

1923

1909

1881

86

1935

1905

1939

1961

1952

1954

1958

1960

1961

1945

1937

1932

1949

1972

1955

1965

1918

1936

1960

1937

1966

1940

1970

1957

1951

1910

1973

1955

1958

1934

1908

1909

1910

1937

ACS

A sketch map of the Chinese railway system

There is approximately 52,000 kilometres
of track connecting 5,000 stations

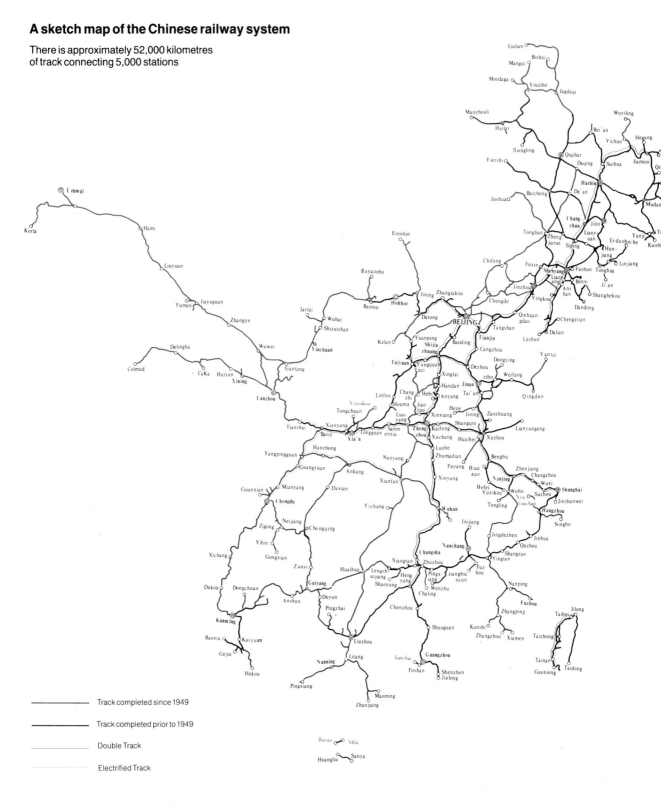

Rarely can an author have received more help than he could have hoped for, but this map is just such a fulfilled desire. The head of the China Railway Publishing House in Beijung, Tu Rongju, knew that I wanted an up-to-date, accurate and informative map of the Chinese People's Republic Railway (CPRR) system. The CPRR timetable contains only a diagramatic map, all in Chinese, so his organization went ahead and produced this map, especially for me for inclusion in this book. My grateful thanks to Mr. Tu and his people. This map will become a source of reference.

Overleaf
One of the last remaining steam-hauled passenger trains in Beijing. 'JF$_1$' class 2–8–2 No. 1208, pulls away from Yongdingmen Station, in the southern suburbs of the capital, with the 13.50 local train to Muchengjian, on 29 October 1982. My guide had rushed me here, from Fengtai, to witness the balancing arrival train and this departure, captured here on my new long lens.

1825, it was nevertheless a turbulent story. Indeed that first line, from Shanghai to Wusong, opened in 1876, and closed in 1877! 'Closed' is a euphemistic description of the event. The line was built by Jardine Matheson and when a Chinese was knocked down and killed on the line it was bought by the Chinese Government, who promptly tore up the track as soon as they had paid for it, shipped it to Taiwan and dumped locomotives, rolling stock and anything moveable, on the beach, where they rusted away.

The Shanghai-Wusong affair highlighted two facts: that most of the first railways built in China were financed and built by foreigners and that, in the early days, railways and politics were closely intertwined. Chinese hostility to railway development in general, and by foreigners in particular, was not groundless. It was felt that such ventures would enable foreigners to penetrate further into the interior and cause trouble; that foreign-run railways could facilitate military adventures against the Emperor; that, as a labour saving device, the railway would remove the gainful employment of coolie carriers and that railroad materials would have to be purchased from abroad, thus draining China of her wealth.

Hostility towards railways slowly diminished, but wrangles about concessionary rights continued, and foreign-owned railways remained a substantial economic and political factor well into this century. Indeed, foreign ownership of all railway mileage, which stood at 41 per cent in 1911 was still, at 18 per cent, a significant figure, in 1937.

Many of the foreign-owned railways in China were constructed for political and military, rather than primarily for economic, reasons. They were built for transporting troops into China, and were used to gain, maintain and increase the interests of their sponsors. Most of the lines were unrelated to China's own economic requirements, but they influenced the subsequent pattern of development of new lines, as extensions and links to the existing railways, were built. Thus the railway legacy inherited in 1949 was far from complete or ideal.

Of the many places that feature significantly in China's early railway history, Manchuria and Tientsin, as they were then known, deserve a mention. The former was constantly coveted by Russia and Japan, and the railways were built at the instigation of both foreign nations. The city of Tientsin, now Tianjin, was always, and remains, one of the most important cities in China. Indeed, with Beijing and Shanghai, it is now one of the three cities meriting designation as a 'city region', or 'Shi', with powers similar to a Province (Sheng).

That first line, from Shanghai to Wusong, the port for

Shanghai, illustrates the drama, struggle and controversy that attended the birth of the railway in China. Indeed, the story of the railway is the story of China itself: a tale of foreign interests scrambling to exploit the new system of transport; of bitter feud between those Chinese who wanted to develop their own railway, and those who favoured foreign loans, foreign contractors and foreign management. Whilst argument raged, progress lapsed, and China suffered. That so little was achieved before 1949 is a legacy of the past. That so much has been done since, is a vindication of the present as far as railway developments are concerned.

'A journey of one thousand miles, begins with a single step', said the late Chairman Mao. Whether this is your first step along the path of the Brotherhood of Rail, or if you are thoroughly familiar with the path; welcome aboard! Let us travel together, whatever our language, our philosophy, our politics or our occupation. Ni Hao!

The barren hills on the borders of Shanxi Province and Inner Mongolia secrete the line that runs north-west from Datong, to terminate at Yungang. The afternoon passenger train emerges from the hills and approaches journey's end, on 30 October 1982. Hauled by a 'JF' class 2–8–2, No. 2157, the train looks like a toy as I photograph it from the hillside overlooking the line. This train is as different from the crack expresses linking China's major cities, as is the 'Flying Scotsman' from a branch line train in North-East Lancashire.

24

1 Class Struggle

This shot, of Class 'JF' 2–8–2, No. 1751 is included for artistic whim rather than educational instruction. Running, light-engine, gently downhill to Datong Station on 31 October 1982, the lines of the 2–8–2 show up well, with the distant hills adding scale to a peaceful railway scene.

Do not worry – I am not about to embark on a political excursion!

For those who are totally unfamiliar with the life of the railway, a few words of explanation of this chapter's title will be appropriate. Locomotives haul trains; different trains require different locomotives, with different numbers and size of wheels. For example, an express passenger train has a greater requirement for speed than an engine hauling a coal train. Thus, each different type of locomotive is known as a 'class'. Usually, but not invariably, it is easy to differentiate visually between each class of locomotive.

China's railways, like those of Britain and of most countries,

grew from small beginnings. Originally, in the last century, individual entrepreneurs, or groups of people in their own community, decided to build a local railway. They purchased their own locomotives. As the inventor of the steam-engine Britain had, and has, a rich legacy of these early locomotives. Over the years, these small local railways expanded and joined up. Eventually a national network was created. Sometimes, steam-engines from ancient classes lived on, still at work fifty, sixty and even seventy years beyond their birth. Old engines to railway enthusiasts, are like old stamps to a philatelist or old jade to a collector.

As modernization and the quest for efficiency became the rule, locomotive standardization became inevitable. In Britain, after the nationalization of our railways in 1948, all new locomotives were 'standardized' in groups or classes. Thus, 'Standard Class 2' engines were used for light passenger trains, 'Standard Class Five' for intermediate traffic and 'Standard Class Nine' engines, the largest of them all, became the heavy freight locomotives. (*See Chapter 3*). Details of the wheel arrangements of various classes can be found on *Page 148*, 'Explanations'.

At Datong, in Northern Shanxi Sheng (Province), is the last locomotive works in the world, still building steam-engines (*see*

Class 'KD$_7$' 2–8–0s are UNRRA locomotives supplied to China in 1946/7. They were built in the USA by Alco, Baldwin and Lima. Those still active seem to be mainly in the Shanghai Region, where I photographed No. 600 shunting Longhua marshalling yard, Shanghai, on 21 March 1982. It was another 'KD$_7$', No. 589, that was brought especially to Shanghai Shed the following day for my visit; the first steam-engine on shed for six years, so my hosts told me.

26

Chapter 9). Their output is restricted to two classes of locomotive only, indeed, now almost entirely one class, the 'QJ', although a few 'JS' locomotives are built here too. 'QJ' stands for QianJin-Advance Forward. As standardization has developed, the older classes of locomotives have been withdrawn from service on the CPRR. Some have found a continued useful life in industrial concerns such as steel works (*see Chapter 10*), but most have been scrapped. In the Class Struggle, railway-style, the old are sadly discarded. Thus, by their rarity, they become magnets for the enthusiast.

In China, railways are part of the everyday scene, not part of the nation's history. Industrial archaeology, as practised increasingly in the West, is in its infancy. Thus, understandably, one's Chinese hosts and friends want to display the most modern facets of their industrial life. Here then is part of the Class Struggle between foreign railway enthusiasts, anxious to seek out and record the existence of the old, the disused and the rare, and the Chinese who, naturally, want to demonstrate the most modern aspects of their railway. However, withdrawals of fairly modern steam-engines in China surely illustrates the modernity of their railway system, and should not cause them to fret when western enthusiasts want to record withdrawn or old locomotives.

It has to be said that British railway enthusiasts are an odd lot! It has taken our Chinese friends a little time to come to terms with our eccentricities. However, my experience of photographing steam in China, has taught me that Chinese friends can quite quickly be enrolled into the 'Brotherhood of Rail'. The glassy stare of incredulity soon becomes the shrugged shoulder of acceptance, the mild inquisitiveness of comprehension, and if you are fortunate, as I have been, the eventual shared interest. You can tell when your Chinese host starts to 'get the bug' as he, or she, learns to identify a 'QJ' from an 'RM', and takes pride in the knowledge gained. Thus "Here comes a steam engine" becomes "Here comes a 'QJ', tender-first." When this moment arrives, you have another candidate for the 'Brotherhood of Rail'.

Life is full of missed opportunities. With my British steam photography I bemoaned the wasted years, when long-lived engines served out their declining days unphotographed. My first visit to China, in 1973, presented me with few photographic opportunities. My knowledge of China's steam stock, was virtually nil. In truth, my interest was fairly low. It was only five years after the demise of steam on British Rail, and I assumed then that my days of railway photography were ended. Indeed, the thought of seeing and photographing steam played no part in the excited anticipation of that first visit. I was totally unprepared for steam.

Overleaf
Undoubtedly the best looking class of Chinese-built engines is the 'JF' class 2–8–2. Without either obstructive smoke deflectors, or those ugly cowlings along the boiler top, masking the chimney, which so distort the good looks of a 'QJ', 'JS' or 'RM', the 'JF' is a handsome, if not elegant, machine. 12 March 1982 was a splendid day up in the hills at Nankou, not far from the Great Wall. Here, Class 'JF' No. 2440 shunts the station yard. Note the cleaning rags, lights and maker's plate above the steam-pipe. Surely a picture for a tourism brochure!

This unreadiness manifested itself in a wild fumbling for my camera as, on the way to the Great Wall, our convoy was halted at a level crossing by a long freight train, headed by a magnificent, gleaming black steam engine. I jumped from the car, ran towards the crossing barrier, and was just in time to photograph the banking engine at the rear of the train. As the plume of white smoke rose up towards the clear blue sky, against the backdrop of purple mountains beyond, something stirred inside me. I had taken my first shot of Chinese steam. An egg had been fertilized.

For the remainder of that visit I took the few opportunities available to me, to photograph steam. I knew not what I saw through my lens. The idea of producing a book would never have occurred to me in my wildest dreams. Now, however, ten years since that first photograph, my research for this book has necessitated a close examination of those early efforts in China in 1973, and they have revealed some gems. Top of the list by far, are the pictures of what transpired to be the last British-built engines to go to China. Designed by an Englishman, Kenneth Cantlie, who was at the time Technical Adviser to the Chinese Railways, they are now in the 'class extinct' category. Their history is told in some detail in *Chapter 10*. Indeed my second photograph was one of these engines, Class 'KF$_1$' No. 4.

The sight of a well-groomed steam express passenger engine, waiting to glide on to the turntable at an important main line motive power depot, is but a memory for tens of thousands of railway enthusiasts. From Zhengzhou to Crewe, Datong to Doncaster, Shanghai to Shrewsbury, 4–6–2 Pacific locomotives are express passenger engines. Class 'RM', No. 1227 simmers gently on Xian Shed on 2 November 1982. Cheng Fa-liang and Liu Wen are perhaps discussing, in the background, the idiosyncrasies of their eccentric British visitor. The 'RMs' were all built in the late-1950s, but are kept in excellent external condition and haul prodigious loads efficiently.

Luoyang 'Shed', a servicing facility for coal, water and sand, was host to Class 'FD' No. 1189 on my visit there on 3 November 1982. She was being prepared for return to her home depot, Guilin, in the south-west following overhaul at Luoyang Works. The Class 'FD' 2–10–2s were sold by the Russians to the Chinese in 1958/9, but are now being withdrawn and replaced by 'QJs'.

Overleaf
The 'JS' class 2–8–2 looks like a shortened version of the 'QJ' 2–10–2. At Fengtai, near Beijing, on 29 October 1982, 'JS' No. 5067 makes use of the last remaining facilities for steam, in the capital. The splendid slogan seems most apt for the steam-engine – 'Vigorous as the morning air, courageously go forward'.

How lucky I was, to see some of these 'KF$_1$' 4–8–4s in 1973. Has anyone else photographed them in China, in service, in colour?

My second visit, in early 1982, was on another Parliamentary delegation. This time I intended to photograph steam, and indeed to create opportunities for myself to do so, with determined persistence, yet I undertook no research into which class of engines existed. After all, I was on a delegation and my photographic forays were, at best, escapes from the formal activities arranged for our group. There was no question of making long journeys to see specific pre-determined places far away from the cities on our scheduled itinerary. Thus again, my ignorance of the details of classes in existence, or their locations, was complete. This will sound like heresy to the hardened enthusiast, for whom my confession is accompanied by an apology.

My third visit to China was a different matter altogether. Planned purposely as a steam photography excursion, I set about seeking information as to where I could find steam at work. This therefore, is the opportunity for me to record my thanks to the magazine that has become my textbook, guide and bibliographer of steam in China, *The Continental Railway Journal* (CRJ). By praising *CRJ*, I hope simultaneously to express to their

contributors, thanks due for the provision of information about China's railways which is not available elsewhere, and to excuse myself for the errors in and omissions of detailed information that will appear obvious to those currently well-informed about China's railways. Ideally each photograph in this book should record the precise location, exact date and correct information on the class of locomotive featured in the photograph. To achieve this, you need to know where you were, on which date, and what you were photographing, plus, vitally, the wherewithall to record this information. If you fail to note all this information at the moment you take the photograph, the chances of subsequently identifying the where, and when, and what, correctly, are not good. Three or even four hands would help, one for the camera, one for the tripod, one for the book in which to write and one for the pencil!

As my books have been noted for their confessions, it is time to bare my soul here. I am not yet expert at the immediate identification of the different classes of Chinese steam-engines. *The Continental Railway Journal* has been virtually my sole source of information and it is written for cognoscenti. This is neither a textbook nor a history book, so I have had to match my own observations, notes and photographs against the information

New railway construction, including numerous bridges, followed the establishment of the People's Republic, in 1949. The sight of a steam-hauled freight, on a misty day, somehow personifies this process. An unidentified Class 'JF' crosses, the River Chan near Xian on 5 November 1982 as the sun struggles to pierce the gloom. Even a city as important as Xian, did not enjoy railway connection until 1934. Xian, known previously as Sian, or Siking, or Changan, had been the capital of China for more than 1,000 years, throughout the Chin, Han and T'ang Dynasties.

provided by *CRJ*, whose main source of information is from foreign railway enthusiast visitors to China. For readers weaned on Ian Allan's abc, with its frequently updated, detailed and precise lists of each locomotive class, individual members thereof and a wealth of aids to recognition, the identification of steam in China is no easy task. If I could read the Chinese characters on the locomotives, my job would be transformed. Furthermore, the engine's own home depot is painted on the tender; in Chinese, too.

Perhaps it might help if I detailed the various classes of steam-engine that I have actually photographed in China, together with some brief notes about them. Again I stress that this is not a text or reference book and I make no attempt here to detail the often numerous sub-classes of each main class. In the light of the shortage, indeed the seeming absence of collated nation-wide information available to enthusiasts about the current numerical strength and details of location of steam on the Chinese People's Republic Railways (CPRR), the following is a guide to those classes that I have seen and photographed at work in China. It should be borne in mind that some older engines are in service in the numerous 'private' industrial railway systems around the country, in steel works, at coal mines or at other undertakings. (*See Chapter 10*).

Before presenting my list I should also say a word about the names of some of the classes; the modern classes having been given names in keeping with post-liberation 'proclamatory' practice. With these apologies and qualifications, here is my list, divided into the main classes now in regular use on the CPRR, the lesser used ones I have seen and those in industrial use. Let me underline again: this is simply a list of engines, of classes that I personally have seen and photographed. The information has been gleaned from conversation, observation and information taken from British publications. If nothing else, it justifies the title of this chapter, if you care to refer back to the opening paragraphs. There is a strong possibility that some of my information contains inaccuracies.

My partner on that memorable visit to China for steam, in October/November 1982, was Ye Weixian, from the Chinese People's Institute of Foreign Affairs in Beijing. His lack of any detailed knowledge of Chinese steam, at the start of our journey together, was soon confronted by his natural thirst for knowledge. By the end of our ten days together, he could identify a 'QJ' from a 'JF', and enjoyed doing so.

To all enthusiasts, the locomotive class is very important. To my wife, an 'A4' is as distinctively different from a '9F', or a 'King' from a pannier tank, as is an omelette from a pork chop.

Overleaf
Only the arrival on the scene in Britain, of the Class '9F' 2–10–0 at the very end of steam, seemed to challenge the assumption of the superiority of the 4–6–2 Pacific wheel arrangement, for express passenger trains. In China, the Class 'RM' 4–6–2 still handles express passenger work in some areas, albeit challenged by the 'QJ' 2–10–2. Back in 1973, the 'SL' Pacifics still had charge of many express passenger tasks. The class is of Japanese origin, some working streamlined in the 1930s on the South Manchuria Railway. There are large gaps in my knowledge of the history of this class. A 4–6–2 'SL', No. 481 rests on Shanghai Shed, on my first visit there in November 1973 during the years of the cultural revolution. My hosts then had a problem, as their eulogy to Chairman Mao praised railway modernization and electrification, whilst I, their guest, had come to admire their steam-engines.

This photograph is included to enable me to mention how sub-classes are numbered. 'JF$_1$' was originally the designation of the Chinese-built, standard version of this diverse class of 2–8–2, many of which were built in Japan in the 1930s and 1940s, and some of which were built in the USA. Indeed, the design originated there in 1918. With the construction in China of the 'JF' in large numbers as the standard shunting and trip-freight engine, the small suffix was dropped. However, some of the class still carry the small '$_1$', as seen here on Class 'JF$_1$', No. 1857, about to leave Xian West Yard on a murky 4 November 1982. The first Chinese-built locomotive was a 2–8–2, which emerged from Qingdao in 1952. Variants include JF$_2$, JF$_4$, JF$_6$, JF$_7$, JF$_8$, JF$_9$, JF$_{10}$, JF$_{11}$, JF$_{12}$, JF$_{13}$, and JF$_{17}$, coming from numerous countries, including Britain. Only Japanese and Chinese-built examples remain in service and they are widespread throughout China.

Class	Name	Wheel arrangement	Notes
QJ	Qian Jin (Advance Forward)	2–10–2	Easily the largest class of locomotive in China, still being built at Datong. Introduced 1956. Total built up to Mar. 82 = 4030 locomotives. Some with 8 wheel tenders, some with 12 wheel tenders.
JS	Jian She (Construction)	2–8–2	Majority built 1957–61, more built in 1965, and a new batch emerged from Datong in 1981, mainly to order of coal and steel users, not the CPRR. Essentially a scaled down QJ.
JF	Jie Fang (Liberation)	2–8–2	Originally known as Mikai class: the earlier locomotives were built in Japan and have smaller tenders. Freight and shunting engine.
RM	Ren Min (Peoples)	4–6–2	'Pacific' locomotive for passenger trains. Built between 1958–61.
SL	Sheng Li (Victory)	4–6–2	'Pacific' locomotive for passenger trains. Originally Japanese-designed and built prior to 1958. Some were streamlined when in use pre-liberation on the South Manchuria Railway. Many variants.
FD	('Felix Dzerzhinski')	2–10–2	Pre-second world war design from the Soviet Union. Being withdrawn systematically and replaced by QJs. Now overhauled at Luoyang Works and returned to home sheds.
KF		4–8–4	Stored out of use since 1976. I saw some in 1973. British-built, by Vulcan Locomotive Works, Lancashire in 1935. (See Chapter 5.
SY	Shang You (Aiming High)	2–8–2	Very few ever in use on CPRR, but still widely used industrially and thus running on CPRR tracks. Two in use as pilots at Xian MPD, probably elsewhere too. Last of the Chinese steam classes to enter service.
KD$_7$		2–8–0	American-built locomotives seemingly now mainly in use around Shanghai, and in industrial use. Introduced in 1946. Variants Japanese built.
PL		2–6–2	PL$_9$ 230 seen dumped at Zhengzhou: PL41 seen at Capital Iron & Steel Works, Beijing.
YJ	Yue Jin (Leap Forward)	2–6–2	In industrial use. Seen and photographed at Capital Iron & Steel Works, Beijing. Mechanically similar to 'JF$_6$' class.
ET		0–8–0 0–8–0T	Polish-built. Not in use on CPRR. I saw a number at Capital Iron & Steel Works, Beijing.
XK		0–6–0T	Those at Capital Iron & Steel Works built in Poland. Some reputedly built E. Germany. Only in industrial use. Similar to USATC engines.
GJ		0–6–0T	One seen dumped at Datong Works. Built Taiyuan, 1959. European design.
Unidentified		4–6–2	In use as stationary boiler at Nankou Locomotive Works. Research has failed positively to identify, but rumoured to be an ex-streamliner from South Manchuria Railway, Class SL$_8$ No. 805.

NB   The first six classes are now the principal locomotives in current main line use nationally.

Fascination with a class has nothing to do with politics! Indeed there can be few less 'political' interests than that of railways. Yet railways are more than a mere mechanical means of transport: they are a way of life. The steam-engine is the heart of that life. Individuality is a feature of the steam-engine's appearance and performance. Comparisons between classes, between railways, between style, and between wheel arrangements, are the subjects of eternal discussion. Was the 'Castle' better than a 'Rebuilt Scot'? Can a 'QJ' outperform an 'RM' on a passenger train? Then the question I cannot help asking myself: how would an updated Riddles '9F' 2–10–0, compare with a Datong-built 'QJ' 2–10–2? That is one of the great unanswered questions of the Class Struggle.

2   The Works

Hand-held camera, interior light and moving people are three features unhelpful in obtaining pin-sharp photographs. However, these difficulties are outweighed by the expression on the face of the chap emerging through the smoke-box door of Class 'QJ' No. 875, inside the Works at Xian Shed, on 4 November 1982.

Even in circumstances of the utmost comfort, and First Class on British Airways certainly merits that description, the flight from London to Beijing is long and can be tiring. If, immediately on arrival, you are taken to your hotel, asked to prepare for, and then attend a formal welcoming banquet, you are ready for a good night's sleep thereafter. As the eight Parliamentarians in the first official Inter-Parliamentary Union (IPU) Delegation to the People's Republic of China sank gratefully into their beds that first night, the thought of the dawn departure the following morning did not delight them at all, except for myself, the youngest member of the delegation. Our destination was disarmingly simple on our itinerary: Nankou Locomotive Works.

I shall never forget the expression on the faces of Edward du Cann, Arthur Bottomley, Fred Willey, Andrew Faulds and the other members of the delegation as we arrived at Nankou. Some of them knew of my obsession for steam, but this was the first time that it had directly interfered with their lives. It was not to be the last on that memorable journey. Suddenly they realized why they were in smart suits, whilst I was in less elegant sartorial attire. Nevertheless, Edward looked perfectly at home two hours later, on the footplate of a Class 'QJ' 2–10–2 and his outward appearance, for the benefit of our hosts, belied his actual feelings, relayed to me. Paraphrasing his assessment of the situation so that his language may be safely read by the young or delicate, he enquired 'Do you actually suppose that we travelled for a long time, and a great distance, and then restricted our hours of sleep in order to make an early start, so that we should be able to share your enjoyment of a form of motive power that not everyone would describe as in the vanguard of technological change' (No prizes are offered for the rather more terse form of words actually used on that occasion by my Right Honourable Friend . . . .)

Whatever the doubts about the attractions of Nankou Locomotive Works, felt by some of my colleagues, I was delighted with the place, not least because the sun shone from a

Rather colourless maybe, but historically perhaps the most interesting photograph in this book. In use as stationary boiler at Nankou Locomotive Works, which I visited on 12 March 1982, this Pacific could be one of the formerly streamlined locomotives used to haul the crack expresses between Beijing and Harbin in the 1950s. It is likely to be Class SL_8, No. 805. Visual evidence indicates this to be a probability, but nobody at Nankou Works seemed able to tell me anything of the history of this locomotive. Indeed they found my interest in their stationary boiler, rather strange; even more strange than my obsession with their living steam engines.

clear blue sky on a glorious, crisp spring morning. Our hosts went out of their way to be hospitable, and the reception on our arrival, from Chang Yizhen and his colleagues, was remarkably different from the style of welcome to which I became accustomed on my previous visit to the People's Republic in 1973. As this was the first formal visit of our delegation's journey in China, I had anticipated, perhaps through ignorance, or perhaps through lack of adequate thought, that we should be received in the same style as nine years previously. Nothing could better illustrate the dramatic difference between the China of Mao's cultural revolution, and the China of the 'eighties, than the reception that awaited us, particularly at industrial locations. In 1973 each and every visit was preceded by a lecture on the revolution, on liberation and on the personal involvement by, and inspiration of, Mao Zedong in the particular establishment one was visiting. Indeed, my admiration for the great man was slightly diminished when the chief engineer at Shanghai engine shed told me that Chairman Mao was personally supporting the programme of railway modernization, including the replacement of China's magnificent steam stock, with diesel and electric locomotives. By 1982, the pre-visit lectures of 1973 had completely disappeared. This was quickly brought home to me, at Nankou, where management efficiency and incentive had replaced political exhortation as the main factor in staff motivation.

This, as I have said, is not a political nor a history book, but it seems in order to pay a passing compliment to the manner in which China's post-revolutionary managers, and indeed their politicians and workers generally, are seeking to evolve a method of social progress that simultaneously encourages efficiency through the use of incentives, yet maintains and develops a classless structure and lifestyle. To compare China in 1982 with Britain, or the United States, or India in 1982, is pointless. To compare China in 1982, with China in 1973 is however relevant and legitimate, and the country can be proud of its progress. Its leaders are conducting a brave experiment in social engineering, whilst grappling with problems of a size and on a scale the contemplation of which can leave one breathless.

Enough of philosophy and politics. Let me return you to Nankou, in March 1982. Nankouzhen lies about 40 kilometres northwest of Beijing just inside a restricted military zone. From the viewpoint of those charged with the task of arranging the itinerary of the British IPU party, it was clearly sensible to combine the idiosyncrasy of Adley with the normal schedule of visitors, by arranging the visit to Nankou Locomotive Works en route to a visit to the Great Wall. Indeed, the station for the Great Wall, Badaling, is not far up the line. As I had 'done' the Wall, I

Overleaf
The major engine-sheds have works equipped for heavy overhaul and repairs. At Zhengzhou, two Class 'QJ' 2–10–2s repose. No. 2755 is receiving the attention of a group of fitters, but No. 3000 is absolutely immaculate after overhaul and repainting. I was told that each driver can select a slogan of his choice for 'his' locomotive, presumably within certain accepted criteria. No. 3000 has already clocked up 1,700,000 kilometres. Across the roof of the works, a slogan exhorts everyone – 'peacefully unite and carry out the four modernizations on a big scale'.

43

naturally asked if I could stay at Nankou whilst the rest of the party went sightseeing. My hosts readily agreed and this was the pattern set for the visit. Wherever and whenever possible, I sought to 'escape' from the rest of the delegation. Not that they were disagreeable, quite the reverse. They were tolerant and indeed it was a most friendly team, splendidly led by Edward du Cann. So it was then, that I had most of the morning to roam freely around Nankou Works.

With the gradual demise of steam from the Beijing area, and the elimination of steam motive power depots from the Capital, the maintenance of steam locomotives in the region has been transferred to Nankou. Although quite small when compared to sheds like Taiyuan North, Shanghai or Zhengzhou, the facilities are quite modern, and Nankou undertakes intermediate overhauls as well as routine servicing and maintenance. However, my abiding memory of the visit centred on my trousers, as I will endeavour to explain.

The patience and courtesy of Chang Yizhen, 'shedmaster', (to use the appropriate English word from the steam era in Britain), seemed endless, but no doubt he was glad when I decided that it was time to leave his Works. Just before entering the canteen, where tea was to be taken, I collected from the car a copy of *In*

Class 'QJ' 2–10–2 No. 918 simmers outside Nankou Works on 12 March 1982. The pride of the railwaymen in the appearance of their motive power, is self-evident. Note that the Chinese People's Republic Railway (CPRR) motif on the front of the locomotive and on the tender, as well as the number-plate and home-base designation, are of metal, rather than painted; reminiscent of the golden age of Britain's railways.

Illustrating both the extent of major overhauls carried out here, and the availability of labour, is this photograph of the Works at Xian Shed, on 4 November 1982. On my first visit to the People's Republic, in 1973, the slogans had been in praise of Chairman Mao and liberation: they are less political, now. Here, workers are urged 'Strictly carry out the rules and regulations and with safe production improve the quality of construction'. Should time permit, they can ponder another recommendation, 'Preserve the character of the working class, show the spirit of being masters and each do his own job well.'

Search of Steam with which to present him. Entering the canteen, my hosts had most thoughtfully prepared two bowls of hot water in which I could wash my hands. Soap was provided, on towels which were draped over the bench on which the two bowls rested. I shall never know why I decided to sit on the end of the bench in order to wash in one of the bowls. The speed with which the bowl at the far end shot in the air, and the unerring accuracy of its trajectory in my direction, was worthy of the most sophisticated electronic targeting. The water just had time to reach me before I collapsed backwards. In a trice I was on the floor, and wet.

The Chinese are not only courteous and polite, they are hospitable and always concerned for the welfare of their guests. I am sure that they would not have laughed had I not done so. Humour was the only answer to such a predicament; not that I had time for a premeditated reaction. As we all fell about, my only comment, seemingly well understood and accurately translated for the assembled company was, 'normally for my acrobatic turn, I perform in a theatre, and charge a fee, but you have have been so kind that I am pleased to offer you a performance here, now, without charge!'

Although I did myself no physical mischief, I had horribly wet trousers. So we set off for the local shop. Nankou, as I have mentioned, is in a restricted area, and the very few shops are not intended to cater for foreigners, let alone Europeans whose anatomical measurements exceed those of the average Chinese. The expression 'fitting room' was not one used a great deal in the clothes shop in Nankou, either. However, with more goodwill and humour, plus the purchase of the largest pair of trousers in the shop, I was warm, dry and respectable again. All this was much more fun than visiting the Great Wall again, especially now that Kodak and Coca Cola have arrived. Give me Nankou any time.

As this chapter is entitled 'The Works', and each chapter title is chosen in order to allow me to select appropriate photographs from my collection, a few words on other works premises seem appropriate. Datong Works, of course, merits and receives a chapter to itself (*see Chapter 9*). Taiyuan North MPD, like many of the larger depots, has its own workshop, but Taiyuan, too, merits a separate chapter. Most of the CPRR workshops seem also, sensibly, to overhaul and repair engines from neighbouring industrial concerns.

Perhaps the only definite disappointment of my visit to China for steam, in October/November 1982, was my failure to obtain access to Luoyang Works. Not included in my tentative itinerary, my wish to visit there was based on the information that it was the sole remaining works at which the 'FD' Class, 2–10–2s were now being overhauled. In truth, my request to insert Luoyang into the schedule, was not particularly satisfactory. Insufficient time appeared to have been available to arrange anything other than a visit to Luoyang Shed. My request to visit the Works on the afternoon of the day we spent in this famous old city, was met with the information that the Works was closed for the afternoon, due to a works meeting. I had to make do with a sight of an 'FD' (*see Page 31*) on shed which had apparently been overhauled at Luoyang Works, and was being prepared for return to its home depot at Guilin.

The Works at Xian MPD saw me taking some excellent shots with a camera, minus film! In addition to my trusty Canon TX, and the new Canon A1 purchased for my specific visit to China for steam, I took with me an Olympus OM2 belonging to my old chum, Dai Woodham, whose famous scrapyard in South Wales (*see Page 141*) now contains the only known supply of unrestored, derelict British steam-engines. Fortunately, I realised that the camera was empty before leaving Xian Works, so I was able to put in a film and retake the photographs. 'RM Pacifics' were much in evidence in Xian Works.

Perhaps I may be excused for ending this chapter with a few

The earliest 'JF' 2–8–2 dates back to 1918. Here, at Nankou Works on 12 March 1982, one of the more recent members of the class, No. 338, simmers under the sander.

more words about that South Wales scrapyard. Despite being private property, with access supposedly controlled by a major nationalized undertaking, depite being unadvertised, it is estimated that more than two million people have made the journey to Barry in South Wales, to gaze at derelict steam engines, now rusted and rotted by nearly twenty years of salt-laden sea air (*see Chapter 11*). In Britain, Barry has become a legend, Dai Woodham a folk-hero, or to some a villain. It is a fascinating tale, the telling of which may illustrate the fact of, but not explain the reason for the fascination that derelict old steam-engines have for those who have succumbed to the spell of the steam-engine.

3 QJ

Anticipation is felt keenly by any railway enthusiast at the imminent sight, sound and feel of double-headed steam-engines starting a long uphill drag with a heavy load. Anyone stationed at the eastern end of Datong, on a fine sunny morning, will not be disappointed, so long as steam reigns supreme on the line up to Julebu. If China was Britain, this stretch of line would have a nickname; probably 'The Long Drag'.

As I have already written, and you, dear reader, have hopefully already read, the chapter entitled 'Class Struggle' (*see Page 25*), it seems appropriate to devote a chapter to the supreme achievement of Chinese steam locomotive engineering: the 'QJ' class 2–10–2. By so doing, I also have the excuse, opportunity, call it what you will, to include here, some of the photographs that I wished to include in this book.

Those people of good taste and judgement who have read my three previous railway books, none of which, unfortunately, has yet been translated into Chinese, will know my limitations. I am neither engineer, technician, draughtsman nor artist. However, the ability to assess a locomotive by its visible performance, is

'QJ' locomotives are widely used on passenger trains. Here, at Shuoxian, locomotives on the Datong-Taiyuan through trains, are changed at the divisional boundary. No. 1185, with flagman, will now proceed to Shuoxian Shed, to be replaced by sister engine No. 2890. This line was originally metre gauge, and in fact was the longest narrow gauge line in China. From here, the line climbs up to a splendid mountain pass, with frequent reminders, for the discerning passenger, of the former narrow gauge line.

The headlight on Class 'QJ' No. 2345 pierces the pervading gloom of late afternoon in Nanjing as the 2–10–2 hurries towards the station, on 20 March 1982. The sight of this engine, as she rounded the distant bend and approached me, and the mournful wail of her whistle, lingered in my memory, and is recalled by my camera. . . .

Right
A long lens photograph of 'QJ' No. 1639 at the east end of Datong, on 31 October 1982. Chinese locomotives seem to have numerous small pipes and orifices through which surplus steam is released.

within my capacity. From the ease with which a 'QJ' lifts a 3,000 ton train from a standing start, it is clearly a steam locomotive ranking with the most efficient and powerful ever built anywhere in the world.

Aesthetically, to my eye, the British steam locomotive engineers built the finest locomotives of their size that the world ever saw. They were the best looking because they had fewer pipes, protuberances and accessories than those built in other countries. As far as railways are concerned I am a British nationalist or, to be more specific, I am convinced that the initials GWR stood not just for Great Western Railway, but for God's Wonderful Railway. (I dread to think how that will translate into Chinese).

When Britain's railways were nationalized, in 1948, it was decided to build a series of British Rail Standard locomotives. Those devotees of the former 'Big Four' railways, the Great Western (GWR), the London Midland & Scottish (LMS), the London & North Eastern (LNER) and Southern (SR) must have assumed that the end of the world was nigh. How could anyone match, let alone surpass, their chosen favourite masterpieces? When the first BR Standard locomotives appeared they were criticized and indeed condemned by innumerable enthusiasts.

'Abandoned' by my guide and interpreter, and scrambling, alone, up a steep hillside overlooking Yungang, near the Inner Mongolian border, I met an astonished local, who immediately helped me to find a good photographic location. With his aid I set up my tripod, in time to capture, through my 500mm lens, 'QJ' No. 2394, shunting far below.

From a bridge across the line at Jianshe Road, in Zhengzhou, I caught this unidentified member of the class, rounding the bend leading from Zhengzhou North Yard, to join the main line east. *Right*

54

As one who dislikes posed or phoney photographs in railway books, let me assure you that this picture was not staged for my camera. The sky was blue, the smoke was white and the engines immaculate. 'QJ' 2–10–2, No. 383 has a pilot for the 27 km of rising gradient eastbound out of Datong, up to Julebu on the main line to Beijing, on 31 October 1982.

57

前进型货运蒸汽机车

QJ TYPE STEAM LOCOMOTIVE FOR FREIGHT SERVICE

中国铁路技术装备公司大同机车工厂

CHINA NATIONAL RAILWAY TECHNICAL EQUIPMENT CORPORATION

DATONG LOCOMOTIVE WORKS

'QJ' No. 1060 has charge of an express freight speeding east past Xian West hump and yard in fading winter afternoon light on 4 November 1982. At that date, Xian remained, blissfully, 100 per cent steam. The only diesel I saw was a mechanical 0–4–0 inside an electrical factory whose manager had responded helpfully, at very short notice, to the request to look at their industrial railway installation. My local guide and I, searching for 'hidden steam', could only collapse with laughter at the sight of the funny thing.

A workaday scene at Zhengzhou, as 'QJ' No. 2754 approaches the bridge that takes Jianshe Road over the railway line. The large permanent way gang wait for the freight to pass before resuming work. Generally, the condition of the track in China is excellent.

No other factory or works, anywhere in the world, can now offer an off-the-shelf delivery of steam locomotives, as illustrated in Datong's brochure.

They were dull, they were boring, they were inefficient and they were ugly.

As prejudice gave ground to perception, and time did its healing work, fair-minded people began to admit that the BR engines were not all bad. By the time that the last new class entered service, people assessed the BR engines for their worth. The last class to be built was the '9F', 2–10–0. It is now recognized by many as the finest, most versatile steam-engine ever built in Britain. The '9F' and the 'QJ' have much in common.

Like the '9F', the 'QJ' is the last steam-engine to be built by their respective railways. Both were designed to handle heavy freight trains at good average speeds, over long distances. Both are ten-coupled, with small driving wheels.

	QJ	9F
Introduced	1956	1954
Wheel arrangement	2–10–2	2–10–0
Cylinders	2	2
Coal capacity in tender*	14.5 tons	7 tons
Water capacity*	40 tons	17.5 tons
Driving wheels – diameter	1500 mm	1524 mm
Cylinders – diameter and stroke	650 mm/800 mm	508 mm/711 mm
Grate Area	6.8 sq. m	3.7 sq. m
Boiler Pressure	15 kgf/cm^2	17.57 kgf/cm^2
Tractive Effort (lbs)	63,340	39,670

* Both locomotives are also fitted with larger-capacity tenders.

Finally, and significantly, both were soon found to be outstandingly useful and efficient at hauling passenger trains, where good acceleration and speedy performance were much in evidence. My journey behind a 'QJ' from Datong' to Taiyuan had something in common with the role of the '9F' on the Somerset and Dorset Joint Railway over the Mendip Hills.

This then is a tribute to the 'QJ'. Long may they serve, and mercifully they will be spared the cruel and contemptuous, indeed contemptible fate, of our '9Fs', some of which were withdrawn from service and scrapped after a mere five years of service.

60

4 The Bridge

Overleaf
The Tientsin-Pukow
(Tianjin-Pukou) Railway was
one of the earliest trunk lines
in China, but Pukou's
significance was solely
related to its geographic
situation, across the river
from Nanjing. Since 1968,
Pukou has lost its importance
as a railway terminus,
bypassed as the line sweeps
towards and across the
Chang Jiang (Yangtze)

Mr. Consul H. King,
in his '*Report on the Trade of
Nanking for the year 1908*'
never envisaged such an
engineering feat, referring
only to the possibility of a
steam ferry across the great
river. On 20 March 1982,
Class 'QJ' 2–10–2 No. 3032
has charge of a northbound
freight at the point where the
road and railway bridges
meet, to cross the river one
above the other. The writing
on the tender indicated that
No. 3032 is based at the
Bengbu section of the
Shanghai Bureau of CPRR. In
steam days in Britain a similar
system pertained, but the
designation was indicated by
number and letter.

Lonely exhilaration gripped me as I set off, alone, across the bridge. China is a huge country, the Yangtze River, in size, far beyond any river in Britain. The story of Soviet infamy in 1960 had just been related to us, the members of the British Parliamentary Delegation to the People's Republic in 1973. The bridge is no ordinary river crossing. Opened some five years earlier, I could not fail to be aware of its symbolizm for the Chinese people. As a young Englishman in his thirties, visiting China during the cultural revolution, I was a little surprised when my hosts agreed to my request to walk the bridge, alone, in order to photograph steam-hauled trains traversing it.

The sheer size of the river, the bridge, indeed the country, seemed to bear closer upon me, as I strode onwards. 6,772 metres long, the bridge carries road and rail traffic one above the other. Striding the tracks, oblivious to everything except my current situation, I kept eyes and ears alert for the tell-tale sight and sound of steam.

Suddenly, I was not alone. Abruptly, my anticipation turned to icy fear. It was not the sight of the swirling river, far below, that caused my heart to miss a beat, as my steps across the planking faltered. Striding towards me determinedly was a member of the People's Liberation Army. His hands were on his rifle.

That moment has been relived many times. I told the story to our hosts when, as a member of the Inter-Parliamentary Union delegation, I revisited the Nanjing Bridge in March 1982. Nothing could better illustrate the liberalization of the Chinese attitude towards foreigners, than the response, nine years after my first visit, to my request to photograph steam-hauled trains on the bridge. In 1973, I was possibly the first person to have made such a request, which was readily granted, albeit probably with feelings of incredulity that anyone would be so interested in steam-engines. By the time of my second visit, nine years later,

the situation in China had dramatically changed. Economic progress, visible everywhere, was accompanied by an easygoing attitude towards foreigners, particularly in places like Nanjing, now very much on the tourist trail. It was with some surprise therefore, that my request to retrace the steps taken during the cultural revolution was none too well received. Clearly, I was an embarrassment to my hosts, not for the first or indeed the last time!

Being determined, thickskinned and not too polite, I persisted. Was there a security clamp-down? Had there been an incident, or yet an accident? 'Why was it all right to walk the bridge and take photographs in 1973, but not now', I enquired.

'Well, to be frank, we get so many people, particularly British friends, coming to the bridge and wanting to walk across it on the railway tracks, taking photographs, that we have had to stop it, purely for safety reasons. There are just too many wanting to do it.'

I can well understand their feelings. The rail bridge really is not designed for sightseeing. Every step has to be watched. It is no place for those afraid of heights. In addition to the planking, and the danger of people falling, there was the additonal hazard of maintenance work on the permanent way, with wrong line

A soldier of the People's Liberation Army (PLA) stands guard as a southbound freight, travelling 'wrong-line' due to permanent way work, thunders off the bridge, headed by Class 'QJ' 2–10–2 No. 2353. By this date, 20 March 1982, most passenger trains crossing the bridge were hauled by diesel locomotives, or 'internal combustion' as they were described by my Chinese friends. The freights however were still in the hands of steam, albeit unremittingly the ubiquitous 'QJs'. Note the guide rails and the standard gauge track; 4′ 8½′′, one of Britain's legacies to the world.

64

Was I the first foreign railway enthusiast to photograph steam on the Bridge? Back in 1973, passenger as well as freight trains were steam-hauled, by a variety of locomotives. Historic interest, rather than photographic quality, qualifies this picture for inclusion in this book. The Bridge is only five years old as piloting 'SL' class Pacific 4–6–2, No. 570 passes the bridge administration office, which is constructed into one of the main pillars, on a murky winter's day, 8 November 1973.

operation from time to time. No wonder the bridge authorities do not encourage random wandering railway photographers. Nevertheless, neither their concern for safety, nor their attention to the rules, could withstand the impolite battering of my ruthless quest for steam. They relented, and arranged for me to return, without the rest of the delegation, the following day.

So, on Saturday, 20 March 1982, accompanied by Wang An-chen, Reception Group Staff Member of the Yangtze River Bridge Administration, I emerged from the door in one of the pillars of the bridge, on to the track. At each end of the bridge the road and rail routes diverge. My first pictures, in the morning mist, were of a steam-hauled freight, high above the river bank, leaving the main bridge and heading towards the misty city. This view brings home forcibly the vital, strategic and symbolic importance of the Nanjing Bridge to the people of China. The infamous behaviour of the Russians, who, at the behest of Kruschev, suddenly halted and withdrew all assistance on the construction of the bridge, is now part of the post-liberation history of the People's Republic. But this is a railway book, not a history book.

History, however, and geography too, invade the mind as one lingers, awaiting the next train. Pukou is no longer an important terminus at the end of the Tianjin-Pukou Railway, one of the

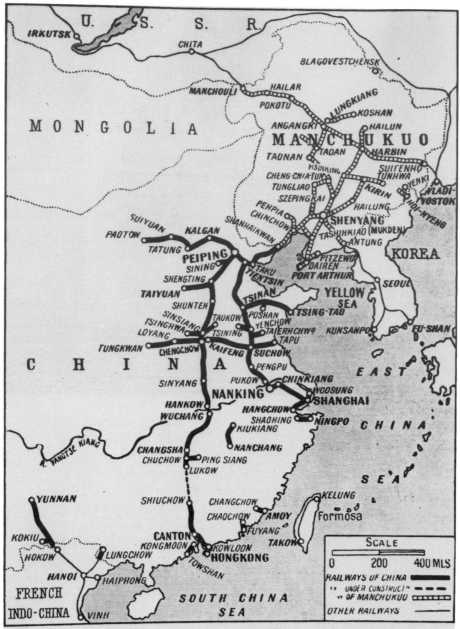

THE CHINESE NATIONAL RAILWAYS operate some 4,280 miles of standard gauge track, and 150 miles of metre-gauge track. The first line in China was completed in 1883. Many new railways are under construction or projected in China to-day.

This map merits a full page for its relevance to this chapter and to the next. Dated 1934, it shows Pukow separated from Nanking. The Bridge was not even a dream. At this date, Nanking was the capital of China. Peiping (Beijing) was uncomfortably close to Japanese-occupied 'Manchukuo'.

The map illustrates, with stunning clarity, the gap in the main north to south railway line ultimately linking Beijing (Peiping) and Guangzhou (Canton), the closing of which was the priority task for Colonel Kenneth Cantlie (see Page 75).

Note the smallness of the railway network, soon to be further decimated by strife. Check the progress made since 1949 by comparing this map with that on Page 20. I am indebted to a constituent who kindly presented me with the two-volume book *Railway Wonders of the World* from which this map is extracted.

Long before the bridge was built, Nanjing, one-time capital of China, enjoyed railway communication, not only east to Shanghai, and north-west to Bengbu, but south to the important river port of Wuhu. This line, the Ning-wu line, was built in 1934/5, and then extended to Tongling, in Anhui Province. On 18 March 1982, Class 'SL' 4–6–2 No. 312 waits at Nanjing's Zhonghuamen Zhan (Station) with the 16.35 train to Wuhu and Tongling. Amongst the interesting details is that 'SL' has become S L (sic), a non-existant roman letter, and the locomotive has what the Chinese called a 'flat chimney', indicating that it has a Giesl ejector. I like this engine.

first and most important railway lines in China. On the north bank of the Yangtze, opposite Nanjing, its railway importance has been eliminated since the opening of the bridge.

Its significance is clear on the map on *Page 66* on which 'NANKING' is shown as the capital city, in 1934. This map, by its paucity of railway lines, shows the giant strides taken since 1949, in achieving the current rail network. (See Page 20.)

Taking photographs on the approach to the bridge provides opportunities to catch locomotives working hard on the rising gradient. But inevitably one is drawn compulsively, back, on to the bridge itself. This time I was determined to walk right across. Wang seemed somewhat less enthusiastic than I, but nevertheless, followed me. The great length of the bridge is hard to appreciate save to say that an approaching train does not announce itself through the transmission of movement on proceeding on to the bridge itself.

The width of the Chang Jiang (Yangtze River) becomes apparent when viewed from the girders at the centre of the bridge. Where, in 1973, the river traffic had been predominantly sail, now there was not a sail in sight. The passenger trains are diesel-hauled. The bridge is now more of interest to tourists, rather than a symbol of heroic nationalism to the locals. The year

1973 seems a long time ago. Indeed, the act of writing this chapter has created the impetus for me to examine in detail, nearly ten years later, the photographs I took on the Nanjing Bridge in 1973. By 1982, 'SL' 4–6–2s on passenger trains, and Russian-built 'FD' 2–10–2s on frieght, were no longer much in evidence, being replaced by a remorseless stream of modern 'QJ' 2–10–2s. The age of standard steam has arrived in China. How strange it is to recall that, in our small island of Britain, the era of BR Standard classes saw locomotives as diverse as 2–6–2 tanks, 4–6–2s and '9F' 2–10–0s, built at Derby and Brighton, Doncaster and Eastleigh, Crewe and Swindon; yet in a country as huge as China, all new steam-engine construction has now been concentrated at Datong: but that is another story. Whenever I think of the Nanjing Bridge, my mind steps back to that long, lonely walk, across that bridge, in 1973. I wonder what that soldier in the People's Liberation Army must have thought as I approached him. Where, amongst 1,000,000,000 people, is he now?

Two days later, I spent three hours on the Bridge itself, repeating an experience enjoyed nearly ten years previously. I never photographed steam on the Forth Bridge, but superficially the smoke swirling through the girders, the bridge reverberating with the weight of the train, the feeling of isolation from 'earth' with the river far below, must have been similar. The length of the Nanjing Bridge, 6,772 metres, gives one ample opportunity to aim the camera at the oncoming train, and to take a series of photographs. Using different lenses on my cameras enabled me to catch the mood of the bridge. Here, 'QJ' No. 2331 rumbles past on a lengthy freight.

5 Friend of Sun Yat Sen

Kenneth Cantlie is a remarkable man, both for his achievements and in his connections. He was Technical Adviser to the Chinese National Railways for eight years from 1930: he designed the last British-built steam-engines for China, the 4–8–4s and he attended Sun Yat Sen's funeral as his family's representative, his father having become a close, long-time personal friend of the great reformer who became first President of the new-born Republic of China in 1911. When I met Kenneth Cantlie for the first time, on Wednesday, 22 December 1982, I knew that this was no ordinary man.

Kenneth Cantlie's father, Sir James Cantlie first visited China in 1888. He was a medical man, with no railway connections, although he numbered amongst his friends at home, C. J. Bowen-Cooke, Locomotive Superintendent of the London & North Western Railway from 1909 to 1920. This friendship was to play a decisive role in moulding Kenneth Cantlie's life, for he idolised the LNWR. But more of that in a moment. In China, in Hong Kong to be precise, Dr. Cantlie received his first group of medical students, amongst whom was the young Sun Yat Sen, not yet 'Dr'. The relationship flourished. Over the years, Dr. Sun Yat Sen and Dr. Cantlie grew very close. Sun was received as a family friend in the Cantlie home in Harley Street, London, where he met young Kenneth. His plan for a national railway system in China was still in the future. The mention of his name, in *HM Consuls Report* for the years 1914–16, highlights the inter-relationship between Chinese politics and railways.

At the outbreak of World War I, Kenneth Cantlie, seeking military service, was declared unfit, having lost the use of one eye. Utilizing his father's contact with Bowen-Cooke he went to Crewe, headquarters of the London & North Western Railway, which he joined, as a personal pupil of the Locomotive Superintendent. So, the man whose father numbered amongst his closest friends the first President of the Republic of China, set

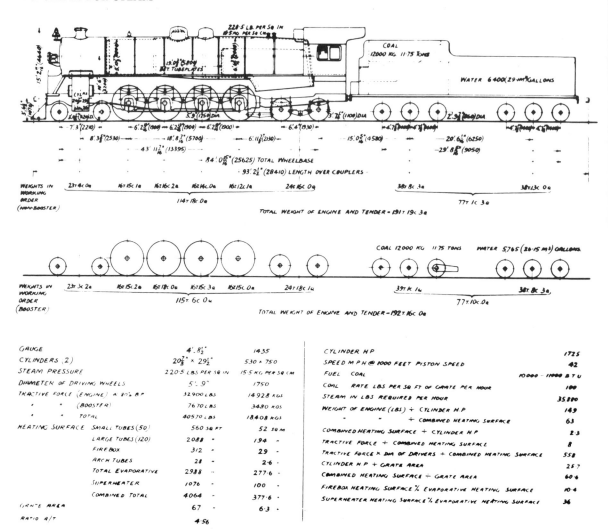

himself on the tracks of a railway career. Some years later, the Cantlie family would renew its links with China, but this time railways, not medicine, would be the bond.

'How did you first find yourself in China?' I asked Kenneth Cantlie, as we sat together in his house in London's Belgravia. I felt like a cub journalist, scribbling furiously as my host, a distinguished elderly gentleman, courteously answered my questions. My attempt to persuade him to compress half a lifetime into half an hour was dictated more by my wish not to outstay my self-invited welcome into his home, rather than shortage of time on my behalf. It is a distinctive tale.

In 1920, after three years at Crewe, he went to Argentina to work on the North-East Argentine Railway, where he spent a further three years. 'Funny people, the Argentines: the Gauchos were OK, but the townspeople were not likeable – not at all.' At that time the British were owning, financing, building and

The technical drawing and specification, dated 1934, loaned to me for inclusion in this book, by Kenneth Cantlie, of a 'KF' class 4–8–4 locomotive. Note the twelve-wheel tender.

Another photograph loaned to me by Kenneth Cantlie, shows an ex-Works Class 'KF' locomotive at Vulcan Works, Newton-le-Willows, prior to shipment to China, in 1935.

Overleaf
Comparison with black and white photographs of Kenneth Cantlie's 4–8–4s, either in service in China, or as now restored at the National Railway Museum at York, highlights the poignancy of the declining days of the 'KFs', in service in China. Had I realised the significance of the locomotive I was photographing, I would have taken more. Albeit encumbered with the paraphernalia of its use, here at Shanghai Shed, as a stationary boiler, the lines of the class 'KF' are well displayed against the clear blue sky. Another 'KF' stands in the background. Walking towards the camera, between the two engines, are my Parliamentary colleagues, Jerry Wiggin, MP for Weston-super-Mare, and Hugh Dykes, MP for Harrow East, who accompanied me to Shanghai Shed on that lovely sunny autumn afternoon; 11 November 1973.

operating railways all over the world and especially in the Empire, as it then was. Kenneth Cantlie's next move up the railway ladder was to India. In 1924 he became Assistant Locomotive Superintendent on the Jodhpur Railway. In 1929, he took some leave, and visited China. He was in the country at the time of the death of Dr. Sun Yat Sen and was invited to represent his family at the State Funeral in Nanjing.

The nonchalant way Kenneth Cantlie related these events could only fail to impress someone with no sense of history, no knowledge of China and no interest in railways. I shall continue this saga on the assumption that you, dear reader, fall into none of these three categories. Amongst those attending the funeral whom Kenneth Cantlie met were H. H. Kung, the 72nd direct descendant of Confucius: and Sun Fo, son of Sun Yat Sen; the former was Minister of Finance and the latter Minister of Railways. As ever, a funeral, like a wedding, was an occasion for renewing old friendships and for making new ones. The two Ministers made Kenneth Cantlie an offer, there and then, to become Technical Adviser to the Chinese National Railways. Neither his family background nor his sense of destiny could allow him to refuse. He took up his post in June 1930.

My trouble is that I cannot stop writing: it becomes a disease. I suppose the natural verbosity of the politician, combined with the inevitable loquaciousness of a railway enthusiast, ensure long-windedness. They also ensure inquisitiveness and perhaps delusions of grandeur. Lest I attempt to write both the history of China and the history of China's railways, let me, in fairness both to the reader and to the authors, refer you to two books that have proved invaluable, but more importantly, fascinating in themselves, as I have prepared this book. One is a small paperback in black and white and the other is quite the opposite. Both are excellent value. If you are so inclined, I suggest you read them:

71

The Railways of China, by Lieutenant Colonel Kenneth Cantlie himself, and *The Thistle and the Jade*, edited by Maggie Keswick. The former is published by the China Society, and the latter is 'A Celebration of 150 years of Jardine Matheson & Co.'.

Having paid my respects to, and acknowledged my debt to two families with such strong links with China, let me return to Kenneth Cantlie, in 1930. His own book tells the tale in much more detail. To me, he described his eight years at Nanjing as 'like a very small tugboat trying to pull the Queen Mary'. Sixty per cent of the Railway's locomotives were out of commission due to the Japanese invasion of China. There was greater demand for traffic than there was wherewithal to provide the service. The permanent way was in a shocking state – 'How on earth it didn't derail the trains, I do not know,' he said.

Kenneth Cantlie had two fundamental problems: funds and priorities. As he talked, he rummaged in a pile of papers, emerging with a thin grey booklet which he gave to me: *The Chinese Government Purchasing Commission's Annual Report*, for the year 1941. Another piece of history was laid before me. This was the report of the Commissioner charged with the task of administering the proceeds of the British Boxer Indemnity Fund. After the Boxer Rebellion of 1900, the Chinese Government had

This photograph is reproduced by courtesy of the National Railway Museum, York. It shows the 'KF' class locomotive presented by the Chinese to the museum as restored by them. The photograph was taken in March 1983.

agreed to pay reparations for the damage inflicted on the embassies and foreign interests. Britain had been slower to put in her claim, and more assiduous in checking its veracity than certain other claimants. What with the 1914–1918 War, as well as China's internal troubles, years slipped by before the claim was settled. Although in the 1920s some of the funds were used to send Chinese students abroad to study, the bulk of the money was intact and accounted for under an exchange of notes, signed between the Chinese Government and His Majesty's Government in 1931 under which it was agreed to establish the purchasing Commission in Britain, with a Board of Trustees in China. Kenneth Cantlie is the last surviving trustee of this fund.

In a nutshell, the Boxer funds were to be used to buy railway equipment in Britain for the Chinese National Railways. Kenneth Cantlie, as a trustee of the fund and of course as Technical Adviser to the Chinese National Railways, was intimately involved. As for priorities, these were clear: first was the completion of the Hankou-Guangzhou (Hankow-Canton) line, part of what should have been the main spinal line from Beijing to Guangzhou. A vital 200 mile section remained unbuilt through the mountains; for reasons unwittingly prophesied twenty one years earlier in the Accounts and Papers of 1909. (See also Page 66.)

Canton-Hankow Railway. – The Canton section of this line is now open to traffic as far as the town of Yun Tam at mile 45, and by the beginning of May the management hope to have trains running to Kong Hau on the North River.

The wisdom of opening the line to passenger and freight traffic before the roadway has been properly ballasted and before the embankments have had time to settle properly is open to question, but the Company are doubtless anxious to give the people of this province a practical illustration of the advantages of railway transport, and also to encourage shareholders to pay up the second call by showing them that the line is likely to prove a paying concern.

Construction is now proceeding as far as section 8, to a point at the north end of the "Blind Boy" gorge, 81 miles from Canton.

The line, which up to section 5 presents few serious engineering difficulties, here enters a mountainous country, necessitating considerable tunnelling and deep cuttings in the rocky cliffs bordering the North River. As in some of the gorges through which the line must pass, the river has been known to rise as much as 65 feet. The difficulty of constructing a flood-proof permanent way can well be imagined.

The "Yueh Han" Railway Company is, I may mention, under purely Chinese management, foreign engineers – British, American, French, Japanese, &c. – being placed in charge of the various sections for construction purposes.

Kenneth Cantlie masterminded the construction, albeit having to settle for a fiercely-graded route made inevitable through financial constraint. The line was built and opened in 1935. This presented Kenneth Cantlie with a formidable motive power challenge of how to acquire engines that were both strong enough to haul 600 ton trains up gradients as steep as 1 in 30 on

the new section of line, whilst not overburdening the bridges on the older section. Thus were his 4–8–4 locomotives born.

I seek not to embellish or repeat what Kenneth Cantlie himself has recorded so well; merely to record snippets of our conversation and to use this chapter as the obvious vehicle to show one or two of my colour photographs of his locomotives, still at work in 1973. Modestly, Kenneth Cantlie shares the credit for the design of these locomotives, not originally given any class name or identification other than 4–8–4, with two Chinese colleagues at his office in Nanjing. The working specifications and drawings were, on completion, sent to the Chinese Government Purchasing Commission office in London. The Chairman of the Commission was the Chinese Ambassador, Wellington Koo. The Vice-Chairman was Sir Ralph Wedgwood. As Kenneth Cantlie mentioned that name, my ears pricked. British railway enthusiasts with historical knowledge, will know why. When Kenneth Cantlie returned to the United Kingdom to supervise the ordering and purchase of his new 4–8–4s, he naturally discussed the project with, amongst others, Sir Ralph Wedgwood who just happened to be Chairman of the London & North Eastern Railway (LNER). At this time, 1934/5, the LNER was in the forefront of steam-engine design, under the leadership of the great Nigel

Grabbing any opportunity to photograph steam, on my first visit to China in 1973, I had not the remotest idea of the identity of the subject. Now I know and realise how fortunate I was. The 'KF' class 4–8–4s were built by Vulcan Engineering Company at Newton-le-Willows, Lancashire in 1934/5, to the design of Kenneth Cantlie, at that time Technical Adviser to Chinese National Railways. This hurried photograph, at Suzhou Station on 9 November 1973, shows Class 'KF$_1$' No. 4 backing down on to her train. 'Shanghai Bureau, City Region' on the tender indicates both her home shed and the probable destination of the train which she will haul.

The number of people disembarking from the train, at the head of which is an unidentified Class 'KF$_1$' 4–8–4, somehow epitomises railway travel in China. Trains are always well-filled. The track layout of the station indicates it is a terminus. Setting this assumption alongside our delegation's itinerary in November 1973, I deduce that the location is Shanghai, and the date 10 November 1973. Note the points operator and the cleanliness. Steam on regular passenger trains at Shanghai is now but a memory.

Gresley, one of whose 'A4' Pacifics, *Mallard*, would soon break the world steam speed record. Indeed, the 126 m.p.h. speed record, set up by *Mallard* between Grantham and Peterborough on 3 July 1938, stands to this day. Kenneth Cantlie is convinced that Wedgwood discussed his projected 4–8–4 locomotive with Gresley: a neat nugget of history not previously revealed.

Whatever the wishes of Wedgwood and Gresley, it was impossible, even if such an idea was discussed, for the locomotives to be built by the LNER at Doncaster. Under legislation dating from the 1850s, all export orders for British-built locomotives had to be placed with the independent manufacturers. The British 'Big Four' railway companies (GWR, LMS, LNER and SR) as successors to the early railway companies, were legally forbidden from undertaking any locomotive construction other than for their own use. So, according to Kenneth Cantlie's memory, the Chinese Government Purchasing Commission put his designs out to tender; to Armstrong Whitworth, to Beyer Peacock, to the North British Locomotive Company and to the Vulcan Locomotive Works of Newton-le-Willows, Lancashire.

The weight of the engines was crucial. Of the four tendering companies, only Vulcan agreed with Cantlie's conclusions over the weight of his 4–8–4s. They won the contract and the first locomotives were shipped out in 1935. Perhaps you can imagine my reaction when, at this point of the story, Kenneth Cantlie stretched across the table and slid to me a batch of photographs and the negatives from which they were printed. They were his working drawings, photographs of the engines under construction at Vulcan Foundry, ex-works photographs of the completed locomotives, and photographs of some of the first shipment.

The first six of Kenneth Cantlie's new 4–8–4s were actually put to work on the Nanjing-Shanghai line, whilst the remaining eighteen worked on the newly-completed Guangzhou-Hankou line, rather faster than as reported in 1910:

Canton-Hankow Railway. – A further 10 miles has been opened for traffic and trains are now running to Wongshek, a market town on the North River, 55 miles by rail from Canton. Construction, however, is practically finished to Ying Tak, 90 miles from Canton, and about one-third of the whole distance to the boundary of the province. Ying Tak is a district city of some importance and the opening of the station there will have the effect of bringing places up the river some three days nearer Canton.

Construction is also proceeding, though less energetically, on the next 30 or 40 miles.

No fast trains are run at present, but a speed of 40 to 50 miles is attained in places by local trains, which cover the whole distance of 55 miles in $3\frac{1}{4}$ hours. The company during the Chinese year 1909–10 carried 1,456,466 passengers and received in passenger fares and freight 294,391 dol. 90c., an average of over 24,500 dol. per month. This amount represents principally short distance passenger traffic and should increase considerably when the town of Ying Tak, above referred to, is reached.

The engines were completely successful. On my first visit to China in 1973 we travelled by train between Nanjing and Shanghai. I photographed the trains, totally ignorant of what I was recording. Indeed, not until my first serious contemplation of writing this book, did I even study closely the photographs I had taken some nine years previously. As is clear beyond peradventure, I photographed some of Cantlie's 4–8–4s still at work nearly forty years later, on the line where they were introduced. What upheavals China has been through, since then. Japanese invasion, World War 2, Kuomintang retreat and finally Communist victory and the end of civil war and turmoil. Through it all, the 4–8–4s survived, as did the Shanghai-Nanjing Railway; one of the busiest in China since its opening on 31 March 1909.

In 1956, as the guest of Zhou Enlai, Kenneth Cantlie returned to China: a different China to that he had left in 1937, but still one where his family's friendship with Sun Yat Sen was remembered. Indeed it was to commemorate the 90th anniversary of Sun Yat Sen's birth that he was invited to return. He met old friends, including F. K. Sah, by now Chief Engineer at the Ministry of Railways.

Perhaps the last word should be about those 4–8–4s. Pending

'Good sturdy Lancashire wheels'. Staff at Shanghai Shed inspect the driving wheels of Class 'KF$_1$', No. 9, in the bright low afternoon sun on 11 November 1973. The red wheels of China's steam-engines are an unforgettable trade mark.

contradiction, let me claim that the photographs on these pages, poor as they indeed are, are the only colour photographs of these engines ever actually printed, whilst in service in China. Scouring the columns of *Continental Railway Journal*, it seems that the first known Western railway enthusiasts organized visit to the People's Republic, took place in June 1976. Amongst the locomotives then seen and detailed, there is no mention of the 4–8–4s. It is stated that 'all passenger trains between Nanking-Shanghai are diesel-hauled'. (*Continental Railway Journal No. 29*, Spring 1977). Another quite detailed report on China, in the Spring 1978 *Continental Railway Journal* still bears no reference to the engines. Not until the Winter 1980 issue (No. 43) is any mention made of a 4–8–4, when it is surmised that the Class 'KF' 'might well be' the Vulcan Foundry-built locos. This is confirmed in *Continental Railway Journal No. 45*, Spring 1981:

KF 4–8–4: The suggestion in CRJ 43 that class KF_1 might well be the Vulcan Foundry-built 4–8–4s has proved correct. In December four of the class were found in the yard of Shanghai diesel depot, KF_1 1 being used as a stationary boiler, 7 ready for shipment to the National Railway Museum, York (it should be there by the time these notes appear), 14 and 17 dumped. A further 17 of the class are reputedly stored some 30km south of Shanghai. A total of 24 were originally built for the Yueh Han (Shanghai–Nanking) Railway, becoming Chinese National Railways 601–24 (VF 9668–83/1935 and 9696–703/1936), but they hardly saw any service before the Japanese occupied that part of China. It appears they were put into store during the war, and three may well have been destroyed, as only 21 reappeared subsequently. They were used until about 1974 on Shanghai–Nanking expresses, but since then have again been in store. These 4–8–4s have been widely claimed as the largest rigid-framed locomotives ever built in Great Britain, but in terms of tractive effort, if not sheer size, are well beaten by the North British-built SAR 25NCs. Are there other contenders?

Note, incidentally, that reference to Shanghai Diesel Depot: a steam shed when first I visited the place, in 1973 (*see Chapter 8*).

Pursuing the accuracy of the comment that they were used 'until about 1974' ties in with the evidence of my own visits. That one of the class has been presented by the Chinese Government to the National Railway Museum at York, will ensure that one of these fine locomotives survives for posterity. As a mark of friendship between Britain and China, and of the respect of the Chinese for the Cantlie family, this gift is wholly appropriate, and greatly appreciated.

Life is full of astonishing coincidence. Whilst electioneering in Christchurch, in May 1983, I knocked on the door of one Dr Cantlie: although I knew this respected local citizen, it had not occurred to me to ask him if he was related to Dr. Kenneth Cantlie. He is: he is his nephew. That afternoon, canvassing was replaced by reminiscing, as we talked of the Cantlie family. They are remarkable people.

6 Taiyuan

Extract from New Atlas and Gazetteer of China (North China Daily News [1920]):

THE PROVINCIAL CAPITAL
Taiyüanfu, the provincial capital.

CHIEF PREFECTURAL CITIES
Tatungfu, the largest centre in the north of the province.
Fenchowfu and Pingyangfu, in the valley of the Fen.

Taiyüanfu. – With a population of some quarter of a million, occupies a position of great natural strength, being surrounded by mountains. It is some 2,500 feet above sea level, and in the valleys leading to the elevated plain surrounding the city there are numerous coal mines. A light gauge railway connects it via Chengtinfu with Paotingfu and Peking, but as yet the enormous coal resources of Shansi province are but little developed.

Fenchowfu. – Some forty miles further down the Fen valley than Taiyüanfu, is also a coal-mining district, but, as the river is not navigable, its products can only be exported by road at considerable expense.

Overleaf
With three engine sheds all having an allocation of steam engines, and with passenger and freight services steam-hauled, Taiyuan presents a railway face to delight the enthusiast. Arriving at Taiyuan Central Station is the overnight 21.49 train from Xian, hauled by 'RM' class Pacific No. 1181, on 1 November 1982. The long lens diminishes colour but heightens dramatic effect. Steam's monopoly will soon be broken in Taiyuan, as is evident by the overhead electrification work not yet energized at the date of my visit. The photograph on Page 90 was taken from the bridge in this picture.

Mr. Xie Li, Secretary General of the Chinese People's Institute of Foreign Affairs, noticeably gulped when I told him that we were going to Taiyuan. 'Really' he exclaimed, and looked inquisitively at Ye Weixian. Confusion however was momentary, ending soon after I told him that our Ambassador, Sir Percy Cradock, had also not been there. It was then that we realised my pronunciation of 'Taiyuan' had become 'Taiwan'! The capital of Shanxi Province, the city of Taiyuan, is significant historically, geographically and photographically from a railway enthusiast's viewpoint.

Few visitors to the People's Republic are fortunate enough to be able to travel to an itinerary of their own choosing, on their own, rather than in a group. 'On their own' does not mean you are left to find your way around a vast country without help. The word 'help' is too modest a word to describe the indispensible assistance of the guide and companion provided for me by Xie Li's organization, the Institute of Foreign Affairs. My companion, Ye Weixian, can hardly have known what was in store for him as we discussed our itinerary before leaving Beijing.

To accommodate all my wishes, communicated before I left London, was impossible in the ten days we had at our disposal, unless, perhaps, if we had had a private helicopter. I think my hosts probably expected that I would ask for that too, and they would have tried to provide it! The proposed itinerary that awaited me on arrival in Beijing, however, was skilfully designed to take in as much, and as many places, as I had requested, within the time available. My only additional request was a little less time at Zhengzhou, in order to add Luoyang to the schedule. This was agreed. I had been told, correctly as it transpired, that the dwindling number of Russian-built Class 'FD' 2–10–2s (*see Chapter 1*) were overhauled at Luoyang Works, and therefore I might be able to see FDs there.

The system of looking after foreign visitors to China is efficient, because it relies on decentralization. Each province has its own Foreign Affairs Office (FAO), attached to the Provincial People's Government. It is as though an English County Council had a department specifically charged with the task of looking after foreign visitors. The Foreign Affairs Institute in Beijing advises the relevant provincial FAO of the date, time, purpose and size of visiting parties, and the local people arrange the details. Naturally, I presented a problem.

Sunrise, or soon after. The 07.25 Taiyuan to Taoxing local train approaches Fenhe Station on 1 November 1982, hauled by an unidentified Class 'QJ' 2–10–2. The combination of long lens, early morning light, and industrial haze make this picture one of my favourites, notwithstanding the inevitable profusion of posts and poles which are both a curse and a challenge for railway photographers in China.

In a nutshell, visitors usually want to see historic sites, temples, pagodas or palaces, rather than engine sheds, marshalling yards, railway workshops or hump shunts. My demands were a severe test of the ingenuity, local knowledge and extent of contacts, of the various FAOs that were on my itinerary. To say that some cities were more efficient and imaginative than others, is not to be critical of anyone or anywhere, because my requests were undoubtedly odd. Indeed, the universal reaction was to do their utmost to please and satisfy me. Where the FAO had arranged for a representative of the CPRR to meet and accompany Ye and I, we were indeed well served.

We travelled to Taiyuan by train No. 201, which left Datong at 11.50 on Sunday, 31 October 1982, and arrived at 19.05 that evening. The train journey started badly, because I overstayed my welcome on the footplate of 'QJ' No. 1185 at Datong Station. The driver seemed to enjoy showing me round his cab and he instructed me in the use of the automatic firebox doors, and encouraged me to enjoy myself with his steam whistle. Unfortunately, I did not hear the 'five minute bell' which exhorts intending passengers to get on board the train. An angry and aggrieved Ye Weixian appeared alongside the cab, on the platform, and took me, reluctantly, to our carriage. His agitation was explained when he told me that the railway rules demand that passengers go aboard the train by the time of the 'five minute whistle'. Ah well, I would not make that mistake again.

Datong to Taiyuan is no trunk route. Originally metre gauge, the line was the longest narrow gauge line in China, before conversion to standard gauge. It is a fine run. From Shuo Xian the line climbs steadily, keeping company, some of the time, with the Hun He (Hun River). We had changed engines at Shuo Xian, it being the divisional boundary point of the railway's operating department. The custom of running locomotives only within their division, seems standard practice in China. As we climbed away on the single track line, one could see the frequent firetowers on the higher points of the mountain range through which we were passing: a symbolic reminder of the Ching Dynasty and of China's rumbustuous history. More recent history was also visible as the remains of the old metre gauge line, its tunnel entrances, river crossing, bridges and trackbed, slipped past the window, particularly as we descended from the summit at Chongxiang. It was a long, hard climb, even for a 'QJ', but, although speed dropped sometimes to 20 m.p.h., there was no sign of adhesion problems for the 2–10–2 locomotive.

The train's intercom kept up a constant accompaniment (*see Chapter 7*). At Ningwu, I saw some semaphore signals, quite a rarity nowadays, and the attendant opened the door on the

Overleaf
Like a snorting dragon, a Class 'QJ' locomotive hauls a freight train past Fenhe, a suburb of Taiyuan, on the misty morning of 1 November 1982. Detailed examination of this picture will reveal another freight coming up in the distance, a man with his bicycle about to cross the tracks, pedestrians, hills away in the background and the inevitable profusion of poles and posts. No photograph can really capture the atmosphere of anticipation that heralds the appearance, and the satisfaction that accompanies the presence, of a steam-engine working hard on a 'real' railway.

85

'wrong' side so that I could take a photograph. We made a longer stop at Yuanping, where I photographed our 'QJ' taking water. As usual, my interest in their activity was rewarded by friendly waves and smiles from the Chinese crew: yet again, a manifestation of steam's essential contribution to the Brotherhood of Rail. At 6.00 p.m. I was encouraged to eat a large bowl of noodles with egg which was delicious. Ye was not certain of the catering arrangements awaiting us at Taiyuan.

He need not have been concerned. On arrival, albeit a Sunday evening, we were greeted most warmly, and amongst those awaiting us was Gao Wenji, from the Railway Administration. Mr. Gao and I immediately struck up an accord. Showing him copies of *In Search of Steam* and *The Call of Steam*, he sensed what I wanted, and we discussed the morrow's activities animatedly. He had previously met two groups of British railway enthusiasts. His name was easily remembered: Ian Gow was Parliamentary Private Secretary to Prime Minister Margaret Thatcher!

Our hosts had arranged a sumptuous meal. After Datong, I had limited my expectations about the hotel, but it was clean, and a hot bath after the long journey was indeed welcome. My friends will evince no surprise at my ability to tuck into another meal. Mr. Gao agreed to a 6.30 a.m. start next morning to search for

Tender-first workings are never very photogenic, but the splendid smoke screen laid by Class 'JS' 2–8–2 No. 5048 entitled this shot to a place in the book. The long lens accentuates and indeed distorts the track curvature as the train runs into Fenhe Station with the 07.06 Lan-sun to Taiyuan local, on 1 November 1982. Note the concrete sleepers and the telegraph-pole on the extreme right; a sight once familiar by Britain's railway lines.

Class 'QJ' 2–10–2, No. 1405 wheels a stopping train from Datong past Taiyuan North Yard on the final stage of its journey 'over the alps' of the Guancen Shan and Yunzhong Shan between the two main cities of Shanxi Sheng. Note the ground signals and the electrification work nearing completion in the Taiyuan area and on the line from Taiyuan to Shijiazhuang. The Taiyuan-Datong line, originally metre gauge, is not an early candidate for electrification, as far as I know, thus ensuring that 'QJs' will continue to work the through trains over this heavily-graded route.

steam at sunrise. My anticipation of the day ahead was tinged with slight apprehension on being told that the journey the following night from Taiyuan to Zhengzhou was to be in a six-berth hard 'bed'. However, tonight was warm and comfortable, and eight hours solid sleep was enjoyed.

Getting up at 6.00 a.m. in the dark, on a Monday morning in November, in Taiyuan, may not be everyone's cup of tea, but at 6.30 a.m., before breakfast, Mr. Gao was ready. Leaving Ye behind, as I am not given to unnecessary torture of fellow human beings, we set off. My request to Mr. Gao was this. 'Can you find a location where I can point my camera straight at the rising sun, with a steam engine, emitting smoke and steam, between my camera and the sun?' Thus we found ourselves not far from the city centre, at a major road junction. Across one of the roads from the intersection, was a railway bridge. It was barely light as I sought a good location. I finished up on the traffic policeman's box in the middle of the intersection, surrounded by dozens of inquisitive, not to say incredulous, Chinese. Where else in the world could one find oneself in such an extraordinary situation?

I suppose if I had stopped to consider my circumstances I might have collapsed with laughter. Goodness knows how many thousands of miles from Westminster, laden with cameras and

Morning departure. Class 'RM' 4–6–2 No. 1182 pulls out of Taiyuan Central Station with the 10.45 to Yuncheng on 1 November 1982.

Overleaf
Old maps fascinate me and seem to appeal to railway enthusiasts. The maps overleaf are included in this chapter only because of its 'geographic' title. The map on page 92 is extracted from the Royal Geographical Society's *Geographical Journal* for November 1898. Changes in spelling are interesting – note 'Korea' or 'Corea'. I like, particularly, the map on page 93, with its clarity and beautiful typography. It is extracted from *Railway Enterprise in China* by P H Kent, published in 1907. There is the world of China's history encapsulated in the phraseology of railways 'Existing, Constructing, Conceded, Suggested'. Many of the latter never materialized.

tripod, accompanied only by two Taiyuanese, I fumbled and stumbled around in the middle of the road, causing a traffic jam of bicycles, buses and pedestrians as I tried to find a good place to pitch the tripod. As the sun emerged through the early morning haze of mist and urban pollution, it was readily apparent that this was not the right place. The bridge was hemmed in by buildings, it was not at the right angle for the sun, and I could not get far enough away to make proper use of my 500 mm lens, which had been purchased for the purpose of taking 'artistic' photographs for this book. Although two or three steam-engines obligingly crossed the bridge, Mr. Gao knew I was not satisfied. 'Let's go,' he said: 'we may have time, before the sun is too high, to find somewhere better. I have an idea.'

As we clambered back into our car, the sun was, by now, well up, although still a good colour. 'I can see what you need, but the place I have in mind is twenty minutes away,' said Gao, via the interpreter. 'Do you want to go there, or shall we go back to the hotel for breakfast?' he asked.

The sun was well up by the time we reached Fenhe Station. This was better, but would have been ideal a little earlier by choice. From the station the line ran reasonably straight in both directions for suffcient distance to enable me to use my long lens. There was an early morning mist and the light, although hazy, was now very bright. It was about 7.30 a.m. when we arrived, just in time to catch the arrival at Fen He of the 7.25 train from Taiyuan to Taoxing. In the opposite direction I photographed the 07.06 Lansun to Taiyuan arriving at and departing from Fenhe, hauled by a 'JS' 2–8–2 locomotive. Freights came by, the sun rose higher, and by the time we left Fenhe and returned to Taiyuan city centre and had breakfast at the hotel, the day had got off to a really good start.

Gao Wenji was superb. He had arranged a busy programme, but ensured that any gaps between appointments were fully utilized on railway photography. We went to the station, by arrangement, and that is not routine, because sightseeing and trainspotting are not normal functions for stations, which are intended for use by arriving and departing passengers.

China is not attuned to the likes, needs and quirks of railway enthusiasts. There are no natives thus smitten! Wherever I went, I found myself the centre of attention, a subject of intense curiosity. It was common for me to set up my camera on the tripod, look around, and the find someone peering through my lens. I did not mind: quite the reverse. My interest in their railways aroused sympathetic friendship.

From Taiyuan Central Station, where we were formally greeted by the station manager, who gave me a CPRR cap badge and suit

SKETCH MAP OF
CHINA
AND ADJOINING REGIONS

Showing the density of Population, Mineral resources,
Chief products, Principal trade routes, Existing and
projected railways, and inland navigation.

Scale of English Miles.

HEIGHTS IN FEET

Reference.
Density of Population per square mile

Products.
Minerals.   Railways.

Limits of Navigation.

Map illustrating
RAILWAYS
IN
CHINA AND MANCHURIA

REFERENCE TO RAILWAYS.

Lines Constructed.

Lines Constructing.

Lines Projected.

pin, we went next to a well-located bridge across the tracks at the southern end of the station. The bridge shook under the weight of the road traffic, creating camera-shake, but the light was excellent.

From here, we went next to Taiyuan East Station, a freight station, where the overhead electrification work, as at Central, was all but complete. From this station I had a tantalizing view of Taiyuan East Shed. Naturally, my feet found themselves tripping across the tracks in the direction of the shed. Although Gao had not included East MPD on our itinerary, there we were. Amongst the engines was a superb old boiler which I photographed. Why are such sights so magnetic to enthusiasts? As we retraced our steps, across the superbly-maintained permanent way, and returned to the platform of Taiyuan East Station, I looked back at the shed. With the overhead wires in place, how much longer would the old order last, hereabouts? We returned to the hotel for lunch as I pondered.

If Taiyuan East Depot had seemed to have a precarious future, my head was soon emptied of such pessimism as we arrived at the city's main depot, Taiyuan North MPD, after lunch. Shedmaster Jin Yuchong presides over a depot with more than 100 allocated locomotives, albeit 'QJ' and 'JS' classes. The shed has the

Beyond the city lies an extensive area of heavily-cultivated suburbia. The sight of a steam-hauled freight threading the fields, gladdens the heart of the railway enthusiast. The setting sun illuminates an unidentified 'QJ' 2–10–2 at Fenhe, near Taiyuan, on 1 November 1982.

I have no idea of the identity of this sad relic, which I photographed at Taiyuan East Shed on 1 November 1982. From such distinguishing features as are available, it may have been a 'JF', perhaps involved in an accident. Who knows? Who cares? ...

capacity to carry out heavy repair work, which is undertaken not only on CPRR locomotives but also on engines belonging to local industrial plants such as Taiyuan Steel Works. I was given the freedom of the shed. Locomotives, taking water, under the sander, simmering, and dead; they were all there. It was just like the good old days at Willesden or Nine Elms, Patricroft or Birkenhead. Taiyuan North has a turntable large enough, naturally, to turn a 'QJ', but operated by a super girl who had to be coaxed into having her photograph taken.

So keen were my hosts to ensure that my photographic needs were attended to, that a stool was provided for me to stand on, to improve the angle whilst 'shooting' the turntable.

From North MPD we bade farewell to Jin Yuchong, and set out for North Marshalling Yard. From here, a further wander brought me on to the main line to Taiyuan from the north. Local information told me that the morning 'stopper' from Datong would be passing shortly. My hosts fretted somewhat as I set up my tripod between the tracks, and got some good long distance and close shots of this train.

By now it was late afternoon. Soon, sunset would be with us. Gao Wenji chivvied me along as we were aiming to return to Fen-he, to photograph in the reverse direction from the morning.

Bidding farewell to the marshalling yard management, we set off across the railway hinterland hereabouts, and, eventually reaching the main road, sped off towards Fenhe, stopping only to allow me to photograph some semaphore signals by the line along side the road. The sun was about to meet the skyline of the distant hills away to the west as I set up tripod and camera for what would undoubtedly be the last photographs of an unforgettable day. We had stopped where the road crossed the railway line. All I could do was wait. The sun reached the rim of the hills, and began to slip slowly out of sight, when a 'QJ' appeared from the west, running slowly, tender-first, towards us. It was not perfect, not dramatic, and certainly not picture postcard material. I was surrounded by the inevitable crowd but, as the sun sank behind the hills, the 'QJ' pressed on inexorably towards me. I clicked away and only time and development would tell to what effect. See pages 8/9.

That was the end of a truly marvellous day in Taiyuan. Back at the hotel I had a bath, packed, rested, and prepared for the six-berth overnight ride to Zhengzhou. But that is another tale.

7

The Railway People

Railway people understand railway enthusiasts, so the natural shyness of the Chinese when confronted by a foreigner's camera, gives way to a friendly grin. The 'Brotherhood of Steam' is alive and well in China, as evidenced here at Fengtai, the last steam stronghold in Beijing. The extensive marshalling yard has steam servicing and stabling facilities nearby, where 'QJs' outnumber the occasional 'JS' and 'JF' 2–8–2s. Here an immaculate Class 'JF', No. 2297, displays its flag-slogan, 'study the Mao Zedong – a model locomotive group'. Note the splendid brass number-plate, too; of a quality not seen in Britain since the splendour of the early years of the century.

Regular travellers, by train, in Europe would be surprised by China's trains as they have a life and style of their own. Indeed, the Brotherhood of Rail is alive and well. As in most countries, the capital city is served by the smartest, fastest and most frequent services. The cross-country lines however, are much more fun, albeit less stylish, speedy and frequent.

Fully to sample a long overnight run, you should travel on a hard berth in a compartment with five others. A foreigner on the main trunk lines from Beijing or Shanghai is commonplace. My presence on train No. 201, from Datong to Taiyuan, was a matter of lively interest to my Chinese fellow-travellers, albeit daytime.

Travelling by train in China, especially on a steam-hauled express, is an occasion to be savoured and enjoyed. To start at the front, so to speak, we have the engine driver, the fireman and, on many locomotives, a third man, the observer, who is responsible, to the driver as a lookout, for signals. The cab of a modern Chinese steam-engine is large and spacious, the crew are friendly and one is invariably welcomed aboard. The roaring fire on the footplate is as welcoming as a roaring fire in the hearth at home. It is alive. There is no more personality to a diesel or electric locomotive than there is to a central heating radiator or an air-conditioning unit. The spirit of steam thrives in China and the spirit too usually pervades the attendants. There are two attendants, usually female, to each carriage. If I say that they act as hostesses, it may be misunderstood. If I say that they are security officers this may also be misunderstood. Their task is to look after the safety, welfare and comfort of their passengers, from checking the closure of doors, to ensuring people have the right seat reservations, and to putting boiling water in the flasks, for the tea provided by the courtesy of CPRR.

It is hard to be stuffy and haughty on a Chinese train. Whether travelling 'soft' or 'hard' class, you are thrown into the company of your fellow-travellers. My good fortune in the autumn of 1982,

学习"毛泽东号"
模范机车组

解放2297

was to be travelling not in a party but on my own, accompanied, of course, by my travelling companion from Beijing, Ye Weixian. From Beijing to Datong we travelled 'soft', in a four-berth sleeper. Datong to Taiyuan was a daytime journey. Taiyuan to Zhengzhou was a journey to savour: a six-berth 'hard', overnight trip. Zhengzhou to Luoyang was a short morning run. Luoyang to Xian was an evening journey, with arrival around midnight. Indeed one only appreciated the train journeys when comparing them with air travel. Xian to Guangzhou was a cramped uncomfortable flight. We had to cut out our scheduled landing at Changsha because of adverse weather and the aircraft, an old Russian machine, was full. There was nothing to make the flight an enjoyable event, save my companion in discomfort. He was a Chinese businessman who spoke no English, but who was learning German, creating a rather unusual 'conversation'.

Let's get back to trains. The life of the attendants is unusual. Unlike the crew of the locomotives, the attendant stays with her train from the beginning to the end of the journey. Our train from Luoyang to Xian was, in fact, the train from Beijing to Chengdu, a 36 hour run and a distance of 2,048 km. Each of the two attendants per carriage does an eight hour shift; resulting in approximately seventeen hours work on the 36 hour journey.

The driver of a 'QJ' in his cab, at Nankou Locomotive Works, on the occasion of the British Inter-Parliamentary Union visit, on 12 March 1982. The circumstances of the visit, and my experiences, are explained on Page 42.

100

'Dimples and Abacus': the lady in charge of the marshalling yard office, at Longhua, Shanghai, on 21 March 1982. As a self-invited guest I was given a friendly and cheerful welcome. There were about ten women working in the office, which had almost certainly not had a foreign visitor before, let alone one toting cameras! My Shanghai guide was concerned about visiting a place 'without permission': but, as I told him, you cannot be refused if you have not even asked . . .

Overleaf
'The Hornblower.' At rural crossing-places, the line is attended by a railway employee, who sounds a series of blasts on the horn to warn people of an approaching train. Here at Mi Jia Yan (Millet Family Village) on 5 November 1982, the shy young girl in her cape, stands with her friend by the black and white posts that mark the crossing-place, as peasants with their mules cross the track. She would not let me take her picture, but allowed me to blow her horn.

I had a long chat with our attendant, Lan Hua. Her home is in Chengdu, the capital of Sichuan Province, and she is attached to the Chengdu Division of CPRR. On arrival in Beijing, on her 'outward' journeys, she generally uses the stationary train as her overnight 'hotel', before commencing the long return journey again, to Chengdu. However, the compensation for four days away, working eight hour on-off shifts, is four days off duty when she gets home. Lan Hua clearly enjoys her job, and she responded to my interest in it by giving me a copy of the first edition of a new magazine called *Railway Companion*, which describes itself as 'The only comprehensive railway guide in China'.

Railway Companion, issue No. 1, is dated 7 July 1982. It is a joint publication by the China Railway Publishing House and the Binoli Publishing Company Limited of Japan. In the quoted words of Li Senmao, Vice-Minister of Railways of the Peoples Republic, 'The publication of *Railway Companion* is not only a new achievement of the Sino-Japanese cultural interflow but also a sign of further development of the traditional friendship between the peoples, railway staff and workers as well as the railway enthusiasts between our two countries.' This was the first time I saw the phrase 'railway enthusiast' used in any

101

The face of experience: Jin Yuchong, Shedmaster of Taiyuan North Shed, on 1 November 1982

'The Turntable Lady': that most evocative of memories of steam engine-sheds, the turntable, at Taiyuan North MPD on 1 November 1982, with the operator holding the door of her hut open in order to pose for my camera. The presence of female staff was one of the few superficial differences between British and Chinese engine-sheds, although I do not recall any of our sheds with the specific job of 'turntable person'. Colour-light signals control access to turntables.

Right
However hard they try, they cannot conceal their charms. Inside Datong Locomotive Works, Wang Yuanyan (right) from the Shanxi Provincial Government Foreign Affairs Department, shares a joke with our interpreter from the staff of the Works. Relaxation has accompanied the end of the cultural revolution, and little items like coloured head scarves are an eloquent testimony to the confidence of Chinese girls to retain simultaneously their right of equality, their status of independent individuality, and their unselfconscious charm, dignity and femininity.

Chinese publication, and I wish *Railway Companion* well if it is able to promote the Brotherhood of Rail.

The average person probably never thinks of the innumerable jobs that are involved in running a railway. Shunter or shedmaster, signalman or linesman, porter or fitter: the jobs are endless, yet each is interdependent on another. Railwaymen and women are no different from other human beings who like to be acknowledged and appreciated. Railway enthusiasts do acknowledge and appreciate the team that is the railway. Perhaps that is why one receives such a warm welcome, as an enthusiast, from China's railway community. Long may it be so.

8 On Shed

Overleaf
According to *Locomotives in China* by Peter Clark, 'JF' class 2–8–2s numbered between 3001 and 3460, are sub-class 'JF$_6$'. No. 3073 runs past the depot office at Xian Shed on 4 November 1982, its multi-coloured appearance attracting attention. I like the 'JF's, yet even they seem cluttered with mechanical paraphernalia when compared to their erstwhile British counterparts. It is strange how French or Chinese, American or Polish locomotives seem always to go in for external extruberances!

My visit to Shanghai Engine Shed, during my first journey to China, in 1973, remains forever etched in my memory. Unlike today, a visit to China in 1973 was a rare experience. The Government of the People's Republic had no such thing as a 'policy for tourism'. I photographed anything and everything in sight. Being allowed to visit Shanghai Shed, instead of visiting yet another educational establishment, was indeed a high point of that three-week adventure. Coming home with about three hundred colour photographs, my aim was to put them in chronological order. I made no attempt seriously to catalogue them. They gave a good image of 'China 73': indeed, together with my Parliamentary colleague Jerry Wiggin, MP for Weston-super-Mare, we successfully persuaded Kodak to enlarge and mount some of our photographs, for display in the House of Commons. The subject, rather than our artistry, was the centre of attraction. My shots of Shanghai Shed were included chronologically in my storage boxes, and one was enlarged, mounted and included in the Kodak exhibition.

Looking again at those photographs taken at Shanghai Shed, my first visit to a Chinese motive power depot, makes me realize not only the extent of my ignorance about Chinese steam, but also the opportunity, now gone for ever, to record, in normal service, the last British-built class of steam engines extensively in use on the main Chinese national railway system. Indeed, all my research, and discussions, have so far failed to reveal any other colour photographs of these locomotives, the Class 'KF$_1$' actually in steam in China. Are my handful of pictures, taken at Shanghai Shed and at work elsewhere on China's main lines in 1973, the sole repository of pictorial evidence in colour of class 'KF's at work in China?

Only a railway enthusiast of some years standing will have personal memories of the old steam round-houses on Britain's railways. We had some wonderful buildings, the atmosphere

inside more akin to a cathedral than a railway building. I visited quite a few Chinese engine sheds, but have not been to one with a round house, although some sheds in the North East contain these charismatic buildings. All the engine sheds that I have visited or seen, have been straight sheds, which makes indoor photography difficult. I have a very strong dislike of 'phoney' photographs: long exposures, artificial lighting or even 'arranged' smoke and steam. However, if interior pictures are not abundant, the shed exterior shot, still is. Turntables and coal stages, sanders and water-columns, all the paraphernalia of the 'home' of the steam locomotive, is still alive and well and living, in China.

This is not a gazetteer of the railway system of the People's Republic, so I shall not attempt to list all the engine sheds that house the 10,000 or so steam locomotives still at work on the CPRR. Perhaps a few words about one fairly typical shed will suffice.

Xian MPD was built in 1935. The main rail access is on to the main line, at the western end of the shed. At the eastern extremity of the shed area, which tapers down to a width of about forty feet, is a gated access on to a siding which runs parallel to the main line. From limited observation, the gate appears to be opened to give the work-force, rather than the locomotives, access to the

Two of Xian Shed's allocation of Pacifics, 'RM' class 4–6–2 Nos. 1121 and 1140, receive routine attention. Coal, water and sand are at hand. The pit is another shed characteristic. Those familiar with the designs of one of Britain's last great men of the steam era, O. V. S. Bulleid, will call to mind his Pacifics through the design of the 'RM's wheels, but CPRR number-plates have a touch of class not evidenced in the painted numbers on the cab-sides of Bulleid's 'Merchant Navy' class locomotives. No. 1140 has one headlight on, to pierce the bright but misty atmosphere.

shed and works area. Plans and diagrams of sheds, such as are available in profusion to British enthusiasts in a multitude of books, are not available in China. This is probably because no one, other than those involved with the operating of the railways, is really interested. After all, I have no interest in the layout of the local gasworks!

Both the Xian shedmaster, Wu Hongliang, and the Chief Engineer, Jiang Chingchang seemed delighted that the Chairman of the British-Chinese Parliamentary Group was so interested in their depot and their operations. My questions, which were not always understood by non-railway people, were readily answered. At the time of my visit, 4 November 1982, Xian had an allocation of 129 locomotives, as follows:

$$44 \times \text{'QJ'} \quad 2{-}10{-}2$$
$$43 \times \text{'RM'} \quad 4{-}6{-}2$$
$$42 \times \text{'JF'} \quad 2{-}8{-}2$$

Of the 'QJs', the majority were with eight-wheel tenders, whilst a few had the twelve-wheel variety for really long-haul work. All the 'QJs' allocated to the shed were in the number range below 2,500. We had a discussion on the numbering policy of the CPRR, from which I gleaned a little more information. The trouble is that one is totally in the hands of the interpreter, who is not a railwayman. With a technical subject such as numbering policy one always fears, and often suspects, that the questions asked and the answers received are sometimes misunderstood. Jiang Chingchang proffered the information that all the 'JFs' with numbers beyond 2,100 were made overseas, but I cannot confirm this from other sources.

Another nugget of information that came my way at Xian is that all Chinese locomotives have the name of their home depot painted on the side of the tender: an invaluable means of identification (if you can read Chinese).

Discussions on manpower revealed that there are 3,100 workers employed in the Motive Power Section of the Xian Railway Bureau. In each location in China, the administration of the CPRR is arranged in regional and area operating groups. Further discussion revealed that the working patterns in China are similar to those applied in Britain during the steam era. One interesting point that emerged at Xian, however, is that men seem not to join the railway as cleaners and then gain promotion to firemen and eventually to drivers. This may be wrong, but it seemed that I was told that 'once a cleaner always a cleaner', and that to be a driver one first joined as a trainee fireman. It takes 7/8 years to progress from fireman to top link driver.

Overleaf
Colour and sunshine at busy Taiyuan North Shed. Detail design differences sometimes accentuate the problem of class identification. Here, I assume that the engine on the left is Class 'QJ' 2–10–2, No. 1535, although the fact that the chimney is visible, together with its shape, makes one consider that it might be an 'FD', were it not for the fact that there is no recent record of any 'FD's in the Taiyuan area. There is no doubt about the identity of Class 'QJ' No. 2891 or Class 'JS' 2–8–2, No. 5048. The wealth of detail and the atmosphere will cause intense nostalgia to enthusiasts for whom there has never been any substitute for a visit to a steam shed.

111

Obviously, shed scenes mean steam and life. Yet, with the standardization of China's steam stock, the chances of finding an elderly locomotive in steam, are becoming remote. Thus a shed visit is an occasion to search for the tell-tale lines of withdrawn engines, amongst which may be an elderly or unusual gem awaiting despatch to the scrapyard. I had heard that there were some withdrawn engines at Zhengzhou.

On arrival at Zhengzhou North MPD on 2 November 1982, we were greeted by shedmaster, Peng Xiaoshun, and taken in for tea. During our discussion I enquired about dumped or withdrawn locomotives, but was assured they had all gone for scrap. Our tour began inside the shed and on emerging therefrom I was asked what I wanted to see first. In a quick survey of the scene, my eye spotted them; a line of derelict engines, tucked away in the distance. Off I strode, rather quickly and very determinedly, with my guide from the Provincial Foreign Affairs Office, Wang Ping. I do not think Peng Xiaoshun was too keen on my rapid march, but he made no attempt to stop me.

There were six withdrawn engines: five Russian Class 'FD' 2–10–2s and one machine that was quite new to me, a 2–6–2 locomotive, numbered 230, and clearly noted as Class 'PL$_9$'. I was told that it was Japanese. For the record then, Zhengzhou yielded:

> 'FD' No. 1180   Withdrawn 1979
> 'FD' No. 1394   Withdrawn 1979
> 'FD' No. 1661   Withdrawn 1979
> 'FD' No. 1772   Withdrawn 1979
> 'FD' No. 1908   Withdrawn 1979
> 'PL$_9$' No. 230   Withdrawn 1959

Shed visits provide a useful opportunity to 'stray' on to an adjacent main line, but on my visit in the Autumn of 1982, my hosts were so helpful that I had no need to trespass. Sheds are usually near stations or marshalling yards and every opportunity to take photographs nearby was afforded me.

Let me end where I began this chapter, at Shanghai Shed. In 1973, Jerry Wiggin, Hugh Dykes and I spent a super afternoon there. When discussing the itinerary for the IPU visit in March 1982, I requested a return visit. This request was fed into the 'machinery' but our itinerary would not be known until we reached Beijing at the start of the visit.

On arrival at Beijing, there was no mention of a visit to Shanghai Shed, but as our first visit, the morning after our arrival in China, was to be Nankou Locomotive Works (*see Page 42*), I did not despair. It was with some surprise however, a few days later,

Coaling steam engines at most Chinese sheds is undertaken by steam crane, operated with speed and precision. Here at Nankou, on 12 March 1982, crane number 203–15T fills wagons. Note the CPRR logo. On the right of the picture can be seen the tender of Nankou's stationary boiler, a photograph of which appears on Page 42.

when I received a telephone call in my room in the guest house at Xian.

'Mr. Adley?'

'Yes.'

'Oh, good. Mr. Adley, I am speaking for Ku Dekong, head of the Locomotive Depot at Shanghai. We understand that you would like to visit us here when you come to Shanghai.'

'Yes, that's right: thank you so much for calling. Will that be in order?'

'Yes, of course. We remember your visit some years ago, and look forward to welcoming you again.' However, there is one thing I have to tell you. The shed was dieselized six years ago, since when we have had no steam-engines based here.'

What could I say? Having requested the visit before leaving London and having been so courteously invited to re-visit the place, even I did not have the bad grace to say, 'no steam, no visit, thanks.' In due course therefore we reached Shanghai, and whilst the rest of the delegation went to see an oil refinery, I went to the engine shed.

Now, as mentioned elsewhere in this book, the difference between China '73 and China '82 was nowhere more obvious than

Taiyuan North Shed on 1 November 1982, with two Class 'QJ' 2–10–2s, Nos. 2632 and 3133, in the foreground. In the distance is the steam shed building, alongside which the new electric facilities were almost complete. Indeed the track in the foreground, to the left of the engines, is equipped with an overhead power line. The water columns and sander, with more steam-engines in the background, provide an atmosphere and a scene once familiar to, and appreciated by thousands of British railway enthusiasts whose thirst cannot be satisfied by servicing facilities for faceless, characterless diesels and electrics that do not even have red wheels.

116

in the style of reception accorded to visitors. This time there was no mention of Chairman Mao. We began, however, to reminisce about my visit nine years previously. It was most agreeable to be remembered, albeit probably for the fact that my visit then, with two Parliamentary colleagues was an exceptional event. Nowadays, foreign visitors to engine sheds are becoming accepted as an occidental but harmless behavioural quirk. Indeed, I tried to tell my Chinese hosts that railway enthusiasts are a potentially lucrative source of tourist revenue, but that is another story.

We chatted about the progress of the railways between 1973 and my current visit, Monday, 22 March 1982. I mentioned that on the previous day, Sunday, I had been to a nearby marshalling yard, in an outskirt of Shanghai called Longhua, where American-built 'KD$_7$' class 2–8–0s were in charge of shunting movements, and handled a number of freights in and out of the yard.

'Are the 'KD$_7$s' not shedded here?' I asked.

'No,' said Ku Dekong, 'but I have something to show you in a minute.'

We chatted a little longer, and discussed the social changes in China since the end of the cultural revolution. As we sat drinking tea, in the rather bare but clean office one would expect at a motive power depot, the atmosphere was really friendly and relaxed. After a while Ku got up, and led me out of the room, down the stairs and out into the yard. We crossed the yard, towards the area of the running shed. I remembered the layout of the place. As we neared the shed, the smell of diesel oil pervaded the atmosphere. My imagination deceived me into seeing a rising wisp of steam over the wall. As we passed through the door into the running area, Ku ushered me through.

I am rarely lost for words, but my surprise was complete. A steam-engine was simmering there amongst the diesels. A Class 'KD$_7$' No. 589 had been brought to the shed especially for me. She was immaculate, and surrounded by inquisitive shed staff who turned their attention to me as I aimed my camera at the visitor. Where else in the world, I thought, would people make such an effort to please and surprise a guest, especially a self-invited guest.

Examining the 'KD$_7$', I looked at the maufacturer's plate, which indicated that No. 589 had been American-built in 1946. My notes seem to indicate that I wrote down 'MCCS Class', but this has no meaning for me, so my jottings remain a mystery. Furthermore, my experience and information does not, on this occasion, tally with the details given in *Continental Railway Journal*, issue No. 50 (Autumn 1982) which states that Shanghai

Overleaf
Xian Shed again, on 4 November 1982. Class 'SY' 2–8–2 No. 1141 blows off gently. The absence of CPRR marking indicates that this is an industrial locomotive, probably on shed for light repairs or routine maintenance. The main points of distinction between the 'SY' and 'JF' class is the shape of the chimney, and the design of the tender. The camera catches the attention of the driver in the cab, and the worker in the right background. At the time of writing this caption, No. 1141 is the highest recorded number for any Class 'SY' locomotive, amongst information collated by informants to the *Continental Railway Journal*.

117

Shed had an allocation of thirty five 'KD$_7$' engines. They must have been at a different shed in Shanghai to the one that I visited, where there were certainly plenty of diesels, but no steam in sight, other than No. 589. Also, *Continental Railway Journal* No. 50 refers to 'a large marshalling yard 16 km along the Nanking line at Nan Hsiang (Nanxiang) with 'KD$_7$' pilots'. The report refers also to a direct line which runs from the west end of that yard, to the Hangzchou line. At the southern end of the other Shanghai cut-off line is the marshalling yard at Longhua, as mentioned earlier. At this location there is a hump shunt and a shed, which I was unable to visit. I presume some of the 'KD$_7$s' are shedded here. I had, however, managed to get into the marshalling yard office. Manned by a dozen young ladies, the place was busy and cheerful, but certainly not accustomed to foreign visitors. My arrival was unexpected, yet the welcome was delightful. Large quantities of paperwork were in evidence, as was the abacus, related to administration of the numerous shunting and train movements in and out of the marshalling yard.

To return, however, to Shanghai Shed, and the title of this chapter, in March 1982, the place was all diesel. When I visited in 1973 it had been mainly steam, with diesels nevertheless also in evidence. Of the photographs that I took in 1973, much the most interesting here turned out to be the 'KF' class of 4–8–4s. The story of these British-built engines is told in *Chapter 5*. At Shanghai Shed in 1973, I photographed one in use as a stationary boiler, and one in store. If only I had known then, what I know now about these British-built engines.

The final shed visit to mention here, is to Luoyang. The sole purpose of including this famous and historic city in my itinerary, was in the hope of seeing Russian-built 'FD' class 2–10–2s under repair in Luoyang Works. I failed in this objective, but managed at least to obtain some shots of an ex-works 'FD' on shed at Luoyang prior to returning to its home shed of Guilin in China's 'deep south'. The Russian 'FDs' are on the way out, being displaced by new 'QJs.' Is it just coincidence that their last active home is as far away as possible from Russia?

Of all steam-engine facilities, the engine shed is the most evocative for the enthusiast. Here is 'home' for the beast, with food, water and shelter. The condition of the locomotives on shed in China is a visible testament to the care and attention they receive; care and attention – and affection? Perhaps not quite as visible as was the case in Britain. If visiting railway enthusiasts to China can infect Chinese railwaymen with our love of the steam-engine, then we can feel that our visits, with all the inconvenience to our hosts, will really have been worthwhile.

9 Datong-Last Birthplace of Steam

Tatungfu. – Is now connected by rail with Peking via Kalgan. It is of little agricultural importance, but local deposits of coal and soda may cause it to become of importance in the future. (New Atlas and Commercial Gazetteer of China [1920]).

Datong is not a pretty place. Indeed, arriving there at daybreak off an overnight train, it is the warmth of the human welcome, and the glow of anticipation, rather than the scenery, that makes life seem tolerable on a cold, misty winter morning. I suppose it must have seemed like that at Crewe, fifty years ago; for Datong, like Crewe, is a railway town.

Ye Weixian and I arrived in Datong at 06.58 on Saturday, 30 October 1982, on the first leg of our journey round China for steam. We were met by Ho Yousheng, Vice-Chairman of the Provincial Foreign Affairs Department, and Wang Yuanyan, interpreter. We had a full day in Datong, with departure on the Sunday morning, at 11.50, for Taiyuan. As we drove from Datong Station to the hotel, we began to discuss our programme. It was to set the pattern for the rest of our journey, and I knew what I wanted – and what I did not want. I had not come to Datong to see the caves! Doubtless the caves are fascinating, but a cave is a cave, be it in France, Jordan or China. Only in China, however, is there the Datong Steam Locomotive Plant; the last place in the world where steam-engines are still built. It is possible that a handful of 'SY' Class engines have recently been completed at Tangshan Works, but this cannot be confirmed. The works were almost destroyed in an earthquake, but some locomotives may have been completed there recently.

Planned in 1954, construction of Datong Steam Locomotive Plant started in 1956, and was completed and the plant operational by 1959. Like many Chinese enterprises on this scale, Datong is not just a place to work. Within the vast complex, (2,380,000 square metres, if you can visualize that) of the production and residential area, are houses, clubs, schools and a hospital exclusively for the work-force. There are 2,200 ma-

121

chines, mostly of Chinese manufacture but including some from Japan, Germany, the United Kingdom and the USA. All this information came pouring forth from our two hosts, Fang Cheng-wu, the Chief Manager, and Chen Beiquan, Section Leader. Of the 8,100 workers, 2,200 are women. There are 180 engineers. The average monthly wage is 75 yuan, plus 15 yuan bonus. Numbers, figures, facts and statistics were produced in profusion, but all I wanted to do was to see the place. Quite simply, there is nowhere else on earth like Datong.

As I write this, alongside me is a brochure. Not indeed just 'a brochure', but the brochure of the China National Railway Technical Equipment Corporation, Datong Locomotive Works and it is the brochure of their main product, the 'QJ TYPE STEAM LOCOMOTIVE FOR FREIGHT SERVICE'. *See Page 59.*

Since mass production of 'QS' commenced at Datong, in 1964, more than 4,000 of the class have been built there. The actual figure I was given, on my visit, was 3,980 at that date. Notwithstanding air-conditioned trains between Guangzhou and Kowloon, or between Beijing and Shanghai, steam is still the backbone of the motive power in China, and more than half of all the locomotives now at work on the CPRR, are Datong products.

In addition to the 'QJ' class 2–10–2s, 'JS' class 2–8–2s have

Inanimate fireboxes that will soon warm to life-breathing fire to power a new 'QJ'. Almost certainly the last steam-engine production line on earth, Datong Locomotive Works has already acquired a mystical reputation amongst dedicated steam enthusiasts: a sort of Chinese Crewe.

been built, from time to time, although there was a lengthy gap in 'JS' production prior to the batch built in 1981, which, so I was told were for industrial, rather than CPRR use.

Datong's customers are each of the six major CPRR Regions, rather than the centralized Ministry of Railways in Beijing. Batches of engines with consecutive numbers are thus allocated to the regions, and the motive power depots within those regions. My questions on numbers of locomotives were sometimes misunderstood, because the word 'number' was interpreted as 'total', rather than as 'individual designation', if you know what I mean. Naturally, my hosts tried to answer my questions, but my questions were more those of a railway enthusiast than a searcher after technical knowledge and information. Perhaps, therefore, I should stop trying to write this chapter as though it were an extract from 'Jane's', and concentrate more on the style epitomised by Ian Allan's 'abc' series. Herein lies one of the minor problems of pursuing the hobby of railway enthusiast, in China. Let me elaborate.

China is a 'serious' country. The problems of feeding, organizing and transporting a society of one thousand million people, are immense. The time available for leisure, is restricted. The pursuit of leisure occupations differs from country to country. Railway enthusiasm, a leisure occupation attached to a 'serious', indeed an essential component of life, industry and movement, is a minority occupation practised mainly, but not exclusively, in Western countries. For a nation like the Chinese, preoccupied with life's important problems, railway enthusiasm may seem frivolous and odd, certainly to many Chinese. My intense interest in their railways was matched only by their intense interest in me! None of this soliloquy is intended as criticism, nor is it my intention to imply that anyone, at Datong or elsewhere, was less than determined to help me to make the most of my visit. The point I am striving rather long-windedly to make is that, at a place like Datong, my hosts were entitled to assume that my interest was more 'technical' than 'atmospheric', yet it was for the atmosphere that I had come.

When Fang Chengwu showed me his 'QJ' brochure, he saw my eyes dilate. My interest and enthusiasm was not however for the technical details contained in the brochure, but more for the fact that I was at a place, the brochure of which was of a product no longer available, ex-works, from any other factory anywhere in the world. Thus was I anxious to reach the shop-floor as soon as good manners permitted.

I am too young to have been to Crewe or Derby, Doncaster or Eastleigh, at the zenith of the steam era. I visited the GWR Works at Swindon in 1963, but by then the era of steam locomotive

Overleaf
Words are superfluous to describe the colourful and evocative magnificence of 'The Works'. These red wheels may seem ostentatious to steam traditionalists, but I think they are quite splendid.

building was over. To say, therefore, that the shop-floor at Datong in 1982, reminded me of Crewe in 1932, is terminologically incorrect, but it must have been similar. I shall not attempt to take you on a 'tour of the Works'. Perhaps one or two pictures may be worth a thousand words; certainly my inadequate words. Perhaps one of my more enduring memories is of the disarming, charming smiles, of Wang Yuanyan (*see Page 104*) and the interpreter from the Works, under their orange safety helmets; not much like Crewe, those two.

The shop-floor space at Datong is immense with more than twenty workshops; steel forgings and pressings, boilers, fire-boxes, coupling and connecting rods, chimneys, and those magnificent red wheels, more Bulleid than Riddles. The working pace seemed none too hectic, and everyone seemed pleased to reciprocate my interest in their job.

To my untrained eye, the Works had the appearance of a series of giant Meccano sets, with a variety of metal objects scattered seemingly at random around the place. Yet there was no suggestion of muddle, just lots of metal. The sight of an enormous workshop, with steam-engines easily recognizable as such by their advanced state of construction, is not one I shall forget easily.

Built at Taiyuan in 1959, 'GJ' class 0–6–0T, No. 1019 lies out of use and rusting, at Datong Locomotive Works on 30 October 1982. Only a few of these engines appear to have been built, and it is obvious that the mania for collecting number-plates from steam-engines, such an obsession in Britain, has not yet reached China!

Outside the Works is the shed where newly-outshopped engines are prepared for their first steaming. One can only imagine the comparative situation say at Doncaster as a new Gresley 'A4' streamlined Pacific had the first fire breathed into her. But the principle of attending the birth of a 'QJ', after the time in the womb of the works, is a time-honoured event now sadly no longer enacted other than at Datong. The first steaming of the 'QJs' takes place whilst the locomotives are in orange primer. Once steaming tests are satisfactorily completed, the coats of gleaming black paint are applied, and the new engine is ready for her emergence from the 'maternity home' of Datong Works, into the big bad world that lies beyond the gates.

As ever, my eyes scoured the landscape for the old, the unusual or the decrepit. I saw and photographed one interesting engine, an 0–6–0T, Class 'GJ', No. 1019, built at the Taiyuan Locomotive Works in 1959.

I could have spent longer at Datong, but the hospitality afforded me meant inevitably that my presence detained senior management from more important tasks. From the Works we returned to the hotel for lunch where there was some uncertainty about the afternoon's arrangements. My suggestion of a station visit was rejected, because a West German railway enthusiast had been knocked down and killed there recently and the local railway administration were understandably reluctant to take any risks with foreign visitors. Foreigners attract crowds, particularly children, and at places like Datong, unlike Beijing, Shanghai or Nanjing there are still relatively few foreign visitors. The suggestion of a visit to the caves was rapidly squashed by my stating, I hope politely but certainly firmly, that I had not come to China for a tourist jaunt, but for the serious business of photographing steam-engines. After animated discussion, I enquired if we might go to the coalfields for which Datong is renowned: the prophecy at the start of this chapter having proved correct. My assumption, accurate as it transpired, was that coal = railway activity = steam. We headed west, out of the city, for the mining town of Yungang, 14 km away.

As this chapter concerns Datong Works, it may seem inappropriate to dwell on the visit to Yungang, but I feel this is worthy of mention. With roads running each side of the river and up the valley, I was reminded slightly of South Wales in the days when coal was king. Less than twenty miles from Inner Mongolia, Yungang is situated, like Dowlais, Hirwaun or Brynmawr, at the head of the valley, with the hills beyond. The huge coalfield, 800 sq. miles in size, contains 10 ft seams of good, hard bituminous coal, just the right stuff for steam locomotives.

My companions found themselves torn between their duty to

Overleaf
Like a cathedral built to the glory of the steam-engine, Datong Works is a hive of activity. Seen here, three 'QJ' class locomotives are in course of construction. In this huge Works, flash-photography would have been meaningless, so natural light and a steady hand had to suffice.

look after and accompany me, and their disinclination to clamber across mountains of coal and coal-dust. The temptation to stay in the car proved too much for them. I always enjoy the solitude of railway photography, but even without my companions I was not alone for long. The locals, hereabouts, clearly found the presence of a foreigner beside the railway line, a matter of intense interest. The smiles made up for our inability to communicate verbally. Merely to step back from my tripod was to ensure that the camera was surrounded. However, even the locals lost interest in me as time slipped by, although children lingered, and girls giggled as I gave them a broad grin. What lovely smiles, and what super teeth everyone, especially the young, have. The level of dental care in China is an example to most other nations.

A fault of the breed of *Homo sapiens* known as railway photographers, is restlessness in the search for a chosen location. Not satisfied with the loading of coal, or the trip workings up the siding to the power-station, I decided that I had to climb up the hillside. Unlike the gentle rolling Dorset landscape, my progress with cameras, case and tripod, was slow and precarious. Even as I climbed a track that barely merited the description of 'path', I met a descending Chinese. Immediately, he offered, indeed insisted on carrying some of my paraphernalia to the highest

New Class 'QJ' No. 6374 lurks inside the Works running-shed, as Works pilot, 'JF' 2–8–2 No. 952 emerges from the shed, blowing off through the chimney. Our visiting party, with orange helmets, can be seen at the bottom left of the picture.

Once completed, the 'QJs' emerge from the works, as a child from the womb, albeit a rather large one. Painted only in primer, they are fired for the very first time. The coal supply for the newly-constructed engines is visible in the background.

130

point which I could attain without going round the hill and out of camera sight of the line, now far below. As he left me and turned back down the steep hillside, I set up the tripod, and fixed my new 500 mm lens on to my faithful Canon TX. I had ascertained that there was an early morning and a late afternoon Datong to Yungang passenger train, and nothing had yet appeared.

They say that the sun shines on the righteous. It was now late afternoon and the haze and mist were clearing to prepare for a fine but cold evening. As the sun appeared, the light for colour photography was slowly diminishing, and my 500 mm lens needs all the light it can get. There I was, halfway up a mountain, not far from Inner Mongolia, waiting for a steam-engine to appear round the distant curve of the hills, far below me. I heard a whistle, I aimed the camera, then, just like a toy train, with the hills all around, a 'JF' with six coaches in tow, rounded the bend and approached journey's end at Yungang. *See Page 24.*

As I half scrambled, half slithered down the hillside, I felt my day had been well-spent. All that remained was to find my guide and companions and perhaps explore that bridge across the other side of the valley, on which a 'QJ' had been standing for some time.

We all met up, crossed the bridge over the river by car, and off I went again, up the hillside on the other side of the valley. By now, the evening sun was bright, the air was clear, and China seemed a splendid place in which to be. After clambering up towards the new line, and surveying the valley from the north side, I raced the sun down the hill, and rejoined the car in time to drive through the village itself before the sun set, the light faded, and we returned to Datong for the night. I was dirty and tired, but happy.

The hotel in Datong gave Ye Weixian and I a yardstick for the rest of the journey. The following morning, Sunday, broke fine and sunny. I had been told of 'a bridge at Datong where you can get some good shots'. As ever, my hosts endeavoured to satisfy my wishes. They knew the bridge and we set off for the place they had in mind . . . but that is another story.

Datong, you are unforgettable.

10 Industrials

Overleaf
The 'SY' class 2–8–2
locomotive is perhaps the
most numerous class in use at
large industrial locations in
China. They are good looking
and efficient engines. Here,
Class 'SY' No. 1034 waits to
collect billets of molten metal
which can be seen being
poured, in the background,
in this atmospheric picture
taken at Capital Works on
14 March 1982. These Works
cover an enormous area, and
the extensive steam-worked
railway system, the molten
metal, and noise create a most
exciting environment, albeit
making the air acrid and
none too healthy. The 'SY'
class, built at Tangshan, was
the last of the Chinese steam
classes to enter production.

The Chinese People's Republic Railway (CPRR) is not the only
arena for seeing and photographing steam in China. Right across
this vast country, but particularly in the more heavily industrial
areas, there are steam-engines at work on the tracks of China's
industrial plants. Indeed, for the connoisseur of the unusual, the
unexpected, or the elderly, China's steel works, coal mines,
chemical plants or innumerable other sites, must present a wealth
of interest. The potential became apparent to me when our Inter-
Parliamentary Union delegation visited the Capital Iron & Steel
Works, Beijing, on Saturday, 13 March 1982.

The sheer size of the place was breathtaking. The phrase
'entering the works', is wholly inappropriate. It was more like
crossing an international border than simply visiting an industrial establishment. It was the reincarnation of the industrial
revolution. My ignorance of matters metallurgical, mechanical
and industrial, prevents me from accurately describing in detail
the activity and scope of this vast enterprise, but one feature was
immediately and abundantly clear; Capital Iron & Steel had a
large, active, and for me exciting, railway system of its own.

Now, on Parliamentary delegations, visits to industrial es-
tablishments are a normal part of the routine. Indeed these
delegations around the world, develop their own momentum and
style. One meets political leaders, visits tourist attractions, and
attends numerous official functions and banquets. At the
meetings, one is greeted formally by the host: then the visiting
delegation leader responds, equally formally, and asks the first
question. At a steel works, questions are reasonably predictable;
about output, demand, the work-force and industrial relations.
Inevitably too, certain members of a Parliamentary delegation
specialize in certain subjects. Edward du Cann, as our'leader, has
interests in steel in the United Kingdom, so he was really at home
at the Capital Works. Arthur Bottomley and Fred Willey, from
Middlesborough and Sunderland in the North-East of England,

133

represented areas of heavy engineering, so their questions were knowledgeable, if predictable. Suddenly, it was my turn.

'How many miles of track have you, on your railway system: do you own your own locomotives and what is the stock?'

Whatever one may say about one's Chinese hosts, it would be hard to sustain an allegation of unpreparedness in the face of questions from their visitors, but it was clear that my questions were not amongst the normal enquiries produced at meetings of this sort. There was a slightly embarrassed silence as each of our hosts waited for one of his colleagues to provide the answers to my questions. It was then decided to send for someone who knew the answers, whilst my Parliamentary colleagues explained my rather specialized interest. Fortunately, the Chinese, being themselves inquisitive, seem rather to enjoy being questioned on unexpected topics, or do I delude myself by mistaking their courtesy and good manners, for pleasure?

As we set off on our tour, by car and on foot, around this enormous place, there were steam-engines everywhere. The other eccentric on the delegation, Andrew Faulds, was my companion in one of the convoy of delegation cars. As he and I were the only two MPs in our group who had been on a previous Parliamentary delegation to China, he was patient and indulgent

In Britain, the locomotive most favoured for industrial use was the 0–6–0 tank engine, an everyday sight too, on British main lines. Such small locomotives are noticeably absent in China, so the sight of Class 'XK' 0–6–0Ts on duty at Capital Works was especially welcome. Some 'XKs' were former US Army Transportation Corps (USATC) engines, and a few of these served in South Wales in 1944, going to France in 1945. It is believed that 20 of the class went on to China, but their subsequent history is unknown. Other 'XK' locomotives were built in Poland and in East Germany in 1957/8. They are particularly well-suited to working in industrial locations, as is seen here at Capital Iron and Steel Works, Beijing, on 14 March 1982.

It seems that I am one of the few, if not the only foreign railway enthusiast to have visited the Capital Iron and Steel Works in Beijing specifically to photograph their extensive railway system. I did this on Sunday, 14 March 1982, following the visit there the previous day by our Parliamentary delegation. It was actually on the Saturday that I saw this unusual engine; Class 'ET$_7$' 0–8–0 No. 503. The 'ET' class of 0–8–0T tank engines are Polish-built, and sub-class 'ET$_7$', as seen here, are conversions from the 0–8–0Ts by the removal of the side tanks and the attachment of tenders. Note the eight-wheel tender, and substantial 'headlight' for tender-first working.

at my frequent efforts to take photographs as the delegation wound its way around the Works. Already, although this was only our second day in China, our hosts and interpreters from the Foreign Affairs Institute, were learning about, and coming to terms, with me and my railway nonsense. It was clear that Capital Iron & Steel Works was quite near to paradise. At the end of the tour, we returned to the reception area where I took my chance to pop the question. 'Would it be possible for me to return here tomorrow, Sunday, for the sole purpose of photographing the railway system?' With little ado it was agreed, and the Chief Engineer of the Steel Works' railway system would be my host.

I suppose there are some people for whom the thought of spending a Sunday afternoon at a steel works outside Beijing, seems some way from heaven. For me, it was bliss. With urgent anticipation, I jumped out of the car on arrival, and after the briefest of formalities, the Chief Engineer and I flanked our interpreter, and my questions began.

'What wheel arrangements are your locomotives?' I asked. The interpreter looked at me, for guidance.

'I don't understand your question, Mr. Adley, and find it hard therefore, to translate.'

I could foresee difficulties here! I tried again, 'How many of

your engines are tank engines, and how many are tender engines?'

Again, the interpreter looked uncomfortable. The Chief Engineer spoke not a word of English, and my Chinese is virtually non-existent. There was nothing for it, I would have to 'draw' my questions. In front of me now are the quite appallingly childish attempts I made, to draw wheel arrangements, tank engine and tender engine, but it worked! There we had the extraordinary sight of a Chinese-speaking engineer and an English-speaking railway enthusiast, quite unable to converse, but understanding each other through pictures, whilst the interpreter, fluent in Chinese and English, couldn't understand either of us. After a few minutes 'education' however, the engineer and I had managed to explain things to him, and we got on famously thereafter. Using phonetics, my notes to myself indicated that 'tank engine' is Ta Sue Sha, and 'tender engine' is Puta Sue Sha. Chinese scholars, please accept my apologies.

On discussing wheel arrangements, it became clear that the Chinese use what I would call the 'Continental' rather than the 'British' system. In other words, our 2–8–2 is their 1–4–1, and our 0–6–0 is their 0–3–0. Surely the British system is best: why count only half the wheels? Having established an understanding on

The identity and history of the locomotive shown here, Class 'PL' 2–6–2, No. 41, is shrouded in uncertainty, and this is not stated to conceal my ignorance. It has been suggested that sub-class 'PL$_6$' tank engines, are British-built. Some other 'PL' sub-classes are stated to be of German or Polish origin. The only other member of the 'PL' class that I have seen, was on the scrap road at Zhengzhou North Shed, where a Class 'PL$_9$' 2–6–2 was dumped, having been withdrawn back in 1959. *See Page 143.* Class 'PL' No. 41 was in excellent external condition when I photographed her at Capital Works on 14 March 1982. It is probable that No. 41 is a Japanese-designed Chinese-built Class 'PL$_2$'.

138

terminology I went on to ask some questions about the locomotive stock owned and operated by the Steel Works. They have 45 locomotives, of which 32 are in steam on duty, 3 on standby and 10 in Works or undergoing repairs. Some of their repair and maintenance work is done at Nankou, and it appeared that a Class 'SY' 2–8–2 that we had seen on the previous day at Nankou, was a 'Capital' engine.

Because British railway enthusiasts are obsessed with classes, numbers and wheel arrangements, I made careful notes of the stock of locomotives, provided as answers to my questions to the Chief Engineer. His terminology for the classes meant little to me, being alliterative translations, the meaning of which I have subsequently discovered. For example, I wrote down 'YTE7' for what transpired to be 'ET$_7$' as written on the cab side of the locomotive referred to, the 0–8–0 tank engines which they operate. The information I was given on their locomotive stock, was that it comprises four different classes of locomotives, the origin of which are detailed below:

Class	Number in stock	Wheel Arrangement	Origin	Date Built
XK	8	0–6–0T	Imported new, from Poland	1959*
ET$_7$	4	0–8–0T	Imported new, from Poland	1959
YJ	13	2–6–2	Built new for 'Capital', in China	1958
SY	20	2–8–2	Built new for 'Capital', in China	1962

* Similar in design to U.S. Army Transportation Corps engines, built 1924–4.

Only the act of writing this chapter, extracting this detail from my scruffy notes, and checking the actual photographs, has enabled me to verify the relevance of the information I was given, and to compare it with the very limited information available, through the columns of *Continental Railway Journal*, of these 'industrial' locomotives. Without I hope boring readers with too much detail, it seems worth mentioning that I saw and photographed all four types, plus an interesting variant, namely an 'ET' class 0–8–0 with tender, rather than a tank engine.

If Capital Iron & Steel Works is any yardstick by which to judge, then China's industrial works around the country are a vast untapped well of locomotive excitement. To contemplate what goodies may lurk unsuspectedly and unexpectedly from Kunming to Ürümqi, or from Wuhan to Harbin, is quite simply, anybody's guess. If only I had ten years to spare.

Notwithstanding that 'Capital's' railway system is entirely separate from the CPRR, it has modern signalling seemingly the same as that on the national system. The locomotives are immaculate, the crews friendly, and the whole railway exudes efficiency. Whereas, on the main railway system, locomotives like the 'QJ', dwarf their surroundings, at the Capital Iron & Steel Works the surroundings dwarf the locomotives. The sight of molten metal being poured, as a backdrop to a railway photograph, adds a colourful dimension. Heat rises from steel billets being shunted by sturdy 'XK' tank engines reminiscent of the 'USA' class 0–6–0T used on the Southern Railway in Britain after World War II. The Company's locomotives work only to the exchange sidings with the state railway system, but CPRR engines can and do work into 'Capital's' premises.

Most CPRR workshops overhaul or repair locomotives from nearby industrial locations. At Taiyuan and Xian, I saw Class 'SY' 2–8–2s belonging to local industrial users. Whereas in Britain, industrial steam engines were usually totally different from the locomotives used on the main railway system, this seems not to be the case in China. *Continental Railway Journal* (CRJ) No. 52, notes that most, but not all, steam locomotives at the locations detailed, Anshan Steel Works, Fushun Mining Administration, Jinan Iron & Steel Works, Taiyuan Steel Works and Wuhan Iron & Steel Works, are from classes in use or formerly in use on the CPRR.

Whether I shall ever enjoy another visit to an extensive 'private' railway system, totally steam-worked, only time will tell. Let the last word on motive power come from Capital Iron & Steel Works Chief Engineer. He has given 'no thought' to dieselization (called 'internal combustion' in China), and expressed himself as 'well satisfied' with his empire of steam.

11

Tomb of the Unknown Engine

'Yet pride there be in death'. Standing stark against the blue sky, on a glorious autumn day at Zhengzhou North Shed on 2 November 1982, an unidentified 'FD' class 2–10–2 awaits her ultimate fate; the last journey to the steelworks to be cut up. Where there is life, there is hope; but in the absence, in China, of any railway enthusiasts to preserve withdrawn engines, and as yet there being no Railway Museum in the People's Republic, there is no future hope for this 'FD'. One day soon, perhaps, railway enthusiasm will flourish, and a Railway Museum will be born. How I should love to be part of such a plan.

The final chapter in my last two books has been about the most famous railway scrapyard in the world. As the steam-engines were withdrawn in Britain, British Rail sold many of them to scrapyards owners. Most of the engines were quickly reduced from proud working machines to lumps of metal: food for the furnace at an adjacent steel works. But, at one scrapyard, at Barry in South Wales, a remarkable and probably unique saga unfolded, through a quirk of fate, which resulted in many of these engines not being cut up. The scrapyard is owned by Dai Woodham, who has become a legend in his own lifetime to tens of thousands of British railway enthusiasts. In the last few years,

dozens of these derelict engines have been bought by enthusiasts and have been, are being or will be restored to working order.

This book is about steam in China, not about scrapyards in Britain. Yet the saga of Woodhams illustrates the strength of the attachment to the steam-engine felt by its admirers and the sight of rusting, derelict engines has a poignancy that defies description in words. Some of those engines at Woodham's at Barry have lain rusting in the salty sea air for nigh on twenty years. Decrepit, disintegrating and vandalized, they yet remain evocatively recognizable, dignified even in death. And so it is with those old wrecks that I have been able to photograph in China.

As the People's Republic has emerged from the long shadow of war, turmoil, foreign domination and interference, the task of industrial modernization has proceeded apace, not least on the railways. Naturally, China's railwaymen are justifiably proud of their achievements. Equally understandably they prefer to display the modern side of the railways. Perhaps not surprisingly therefore, they are unenthusiastic about one's interest in withdrawn and rusting hulks of locomotives, reminders of the past, rather than evidence of the present.

My interest in old locomotives is engendered in the same soil that fertilizes the interest of the philatelist in old postage stamps. I

My poetry has attracted adverse and well-deserved criticism, both the 'railway' and the 'political' variety, so I shall resist the temptation to wax lyrical in verse at the sight shown here. It has become traditional for the last chapter in my railway books to comprise photographs of dead engines rusting away and awaiting scrapping. Here at Zhengzhou, Russian-built 'FD' class 2–10–2, No. 1908 lingers on the scrap line, having been withdrawn in 1979. It is fitted with a Giesl ejector, judging by the shape of the chimney. These engines were described to me as 'Russian trash' by one of my railway hosts at Zhengzhou Shed. What a difference the sun makes, to railway photography.

Class 'PL$_9$' 2–6–2, No. 230 had already languished on the scrap line at Zhengzhou North Shed for 23 years when I took this photograph, on 2 November 1982. For some reason she had escaped the cutters torch, and stood amongst a batch of 'FD' 2–10–2s, awaiting their fate. This is a particularly interesting engine, built by Skoda in 1937. The sight of condemned engines transcends national, ethnic and cultural barriers in its nostalgic appeal to true railway enthusiasts.

Overleaf
Scraps of fading red paint are overwhelmed by the pervasive rust on this derelict 2–10–2 locomotive, seen at Taiyuan North Shed on 1 November 1982. Information about its background was not available, but the phrase 'an old Russian', used by my host, identifies it as an 'FD'. Neither rust nor dereliction can rob a locomotive of her dignity, which seems somehow to be captured here. "Someone save me" she whispered, as I walked slowly past . . . or was it the wind?

hope that my credentials as a friend of China, will explain my interest, indeed some might say morbid curiosity, in their old, withdrawn engines. In fact, the very speed of their railway modernization programme means that even some comparatively young steam-engines have already been withdrawn. The scope for capturing on film, for posterity, old locomotives in China, is very limited. They have nearly all gone already. Whereas, in Britain, some very old locomotives served British Rail almost up to the end of steam, there are few, if any, ancient steam-engines still in service on the CPRR.

With the presentation of Class 'KF$_1$' No. 7 to the National Railway Museum in York, I wonder if the Chinese People's Republic Railways will do for themselves, what they have so kindly and generously done for us here in Britain. By recognizing the importance to us, that old British-built locomotives represent in terms of our industrial archaeology, will they start to prepare for themselves a National collection of their own? Surely it would be unthinkable if there were no plan for a Chinese Railway Museum. Indeed the very recognition of the importance of such a display would itself be a recognition of the status of China as an industrially-advancing and competent country.

Let me not end this chapter, or indeed this book, on an

143

academic note. Let me take you back to Dai Woodham's scrapyard in South Wales. The great saga of Woodhams has been the almost miraculous rescue, and restoration of so many scrapped, derelict and rusting engines, to working order. Many an abandoned engine is now living; literally living testimony to the spirit of steam enthusiasts. Up and down Britain, preserved railways, run by enthusiasts, have sprung to life again. Where there is metal, there is hope. Will any of China's withdrawn and rusting engines be restored, somewhere, sometime, by someone?

Let us hope so.

Abbreviations

The use of initials, in place of the full name or title of bodies and organizations, is a disease. Those worst afflicted are politicians, civil servants and railway enthusiasts; to name but three. These abbreviations are useful, but can be extremely worrying when used without adequate explanation. I have tried to avoid too many, and have sought, when I have remembered, only to use initials after the name has been written in full.

The initials most frequently used are CPRR: they stand for Chinese People's Republic Railway. Strangely, I have been unable to find confirmation that these initials are acceptable to the Chinese. There is presumably a Pinyin version of 'Chinese People's Republic Railway' but if there is a romanized set of initials for the national railway system, my searches and conversations have not uncovered a set of initials universally adopted and in use.

Happily, my list is brief.

ABBREVIATIONS

BR   –   British Rail
CPRR   –   Chinese People's Republic Railway
CRJ   –   Continental Railway Journal
GWR   –   Great Western Railway
IPU   –   Inter-Parliamentary Union
LMS   –   London Midland & Scottish Railway
LNER   –   London & North Eastern Railway
LNWR   –   London & North Western Railway
MOD   –   Ministry of Defence
MPD   –   Motive Power Depot (Engine Shed)
OS   –   Ordnance Survey
PLA   –   Peoples Liberation Army
RGS   –   Royal Geographical Society
SR   –   Southern Railway
UNRRA –   United Nations Relief and Rehabilitation Administration
USATC –   United States Army Transportation Corps

Explanations

Each separate class of Chinese steam-engine is described by a two-letter classification. The designation of each class is based on two syllables, chosen to identify each separate class. This system itself is derived from the system applied by the Japanese during their occupation of China. The actual choice of individual class names, and their identifying letters, has evolved from a variety of sources, some based on traditional American-type names, but the more modern Chinese-built locos are named on a 'revolutionary', 'heroic' or 'political' basis. These are listed in the chart on page 39, and are repeated here.

胜利	SHENGLI (SL Type)	VICTORY
跃进	YUEJIN (YJ Type)	LEAP FORWARD
上游	SHANGYOU (SY Type)	AIMING HIGH
人民	RENMIN (RM Type)	PEOPLE'S
前进	QIANJIN (QJ Type)	ADVANCE FORWARD
解放	JIEFANG (JF Type)	LIBERATION
建设	JIANSHE (JS Type)	CONSTRUCTION

Throughout this book, the reader will have met the phrase 'wheel arrangement' as well as the frequent use of the two-letter classification mentioned above. I hope the following chart will explain the terminology, which is an international language to railwaymen and to railway enthusiasts.

Note: Locomotives of a 4–6–2 wheel arrangement are commonly designated as 'Pacific' locomotives. Other, less commonly-used names are not listed, to avoid confusion.

Wheel-Arrangement		Designation	Class(es)
o o o	=	0–6–0	XK:GJ
o o O o o	=	2–6–2	PL:YJ
o o O o o o	=	4–6–2	SL:RM
o o o o	=	0–8–0	ET
o o o o o	=	2–8–0	KD
o o o o o o	=	2–8–2	JF:JS:SY
o o o o o o o o	=	4–8–4	KF
o o o o o o o	=	2–10–2	FD:QJ

There are other methods used to describe the wheel arrangement (see Page 39). To describe in detail would serve only to confuse.

The other word used which also confuses those unfamiliar with railway parlance is the word 'tank'. There are no military connotations here! Steam-engines carry coal and water. Usually they are in a 'tender' attached to the engine itself. However, small locomotives are often used for shunting or short-distance work, or when the absence of turning facilities requires 'backward' running of locomotives. For this work, tank engines are more suitable: the coal being carried in a bunker behind the cab and the water in tanks alongside the boiler. The 'T' after the wheel arrangement denotes a tank engine.

Locomotives with a tender, as are virtually all locomotives in China today, are seen to be running 'tender first' when running 'backwards'. In this position they are not very photogenic.

One final 'explanation' is the use of the word 'shed'. This word, or the phrase 'Motive Power Depot' (MPD) refers to the building where engines are based, from which they work and to which they return at the end of each duty. At the shed are coal, water, sand: the daily requirements of the working steam-engine.

There are doubtless other words that I have used in the text, which may cause you to scratch your head: words like 'banking', which has nothing to do with capitalism, but describes the activity of an engine helping to push a heavy train up a steep bank: or 'double-heading', which is not a freak of birth, but describes the use of two locomotives at the head of a train. I hope I may be forgiven for omissions of more explanatory terms and that such omissions do not detract from your enjoyment of this book.

Transliterations

What is Pinyin? What is Wade-Giles?
They are two entirely different methods of achieving a similar objective; namely, to represent the sounds of the Chinese language alphabetically in Roman letters. In a phrase, the romanization of Chinese.

Wade-Giles was a system created by foreigners, to enable foreigners to pronounce Chinese, and to be able to refer to names in common use.

Pinyin, which is short for Hanyu Pinyin, means 'phonetic transcription of the Chinese language.' In contradistinction to Wade-Giles, it is a system introduced by the Chinese in 1958. It was not created by or for Englishmen. It is used for teaching young children, in dialect areas, the standard pronunciation of Chinese. Written Chinese is uniform throughout China, but the spoken language varies from one region to the next and there are eight major dialect groups. As the Chinese language comprises 'characters' rather than 'letters', it has no written phonetic alphabet. As I have said on page 17, it seems right to endeavour to use Pinyin, rather than Wade-Giles, throughout this book. Pinyin is the system of the present and the future: Wade-Giles, is of the past. Direct references from or to old maps and documents are, however, written or quoted in their original form. Brackets are used where appropriate.

This book is not an educational tome and it is bound to contain mistakes. Penny Brooke at the Great Britain-China Centre in London has done her best to put me on the right road. If you refer to page 17 you can just begin to appreciate the problems. Some of the most widely-differing letters between Wade-Giles and Pinyin (Wade-Giles first) are: hs = x; ch' = q; ch = zh; ts = z; ts' = c; j = r; tz = z. I am setting this out merely to illustrate the problem. That is my excuse for any mistakes of this nature found in the text. Here are some of the transliterations from the text which may be useful.

150

Pinyin		Wade-Giles (or traditional)
Beijing	—	Peking
Bengbu	—	Pengpu
Chang Jiang	—	Yangtze
Chengdu	—	Cheng-tu
Chongqing	—	Chungking
Datong	—	Tat'ung
Fengtai	—	Fengt'ai
Guangzhou	—	(Canton)
Guilin	—	Kweilin
Hangzhou	—	Hangchow
Jinan	—	Tsinan
Hankou	—	Hankow
Lüda (Dalian)	—	Dairen
Luoyang	—	Loyang
Mao Zedong	—	Mao Tse-tung
Menggu	—	(Mongolia)
Nanjing	—	Nanking
Nankou	—	Nankou
Nanxiang	—	Nan Hsiang
Pukou	—	Pukow
Qingdao	—	(Tsingtao)
Shaanxi	—	Shensi
Shanxi	—	Shansi
Shijiazhuang	—	Shihchiachuan (Shihkiachwang)
Shuo Xian	—	Shuo-hsien
Sichuán	—	Szechuan
Suzhou	—	Soochow
Taiyuan	—	T'ai-yuan (Taiyuen)
Tangshan	—	Tangshan
Tianjin	—	Tientsin
Tongling	—	Tungling
Wuhan	—	Formerly the three cities of Hankow, Hanyang and Wuchang.
Wusong	—	Wu-sung
Xian*	—	Sian (Hsi-an; Siking)
Yungang	—	Yun Kang
Xizang	—	(Tibet)
Zhangjiakou	—	(Kalgan)
Zhengzhou	—	Chengchow
Zhou Enlai	—	Chou En-Lai

* Correctly written: Xi'an, but common usage: Xian

Index

People and places mentioned in the main text, and in the captions, are included in this Index. Locomotives are not indexed: nor is the Chinese People's Republic Railway (CPRR) due to frequent repetition.